Ten Reasons

Proposed To His Adversaries For Disputation In The Name Of The Faith And Presented To The Illustrious Members Of Our Universities

Edmund Campion

Alpha Editions

This edition published in 2021

ISBN : 9789354411489

Design and Setting By
Alpha Editions
www.alphaedis.com
Email - info@alphaedis.com

As per information held with us this book is in Public Domain.
This book is a reproduction of an important historical work. Alpha Editions uses the best technology to reproduce historical work in the same manner it was first published to preserve its original nature. Any marks or number seen are left intentionally to preserve its true form.

CONTENTS.

INTRODUCTION I

RATIONES DECEM 30

TRANSLATION 88

INTRODUCTION.

THOUGH Blessed Edmund Campion's *Decem Rationes* has passed through forty-seven editions,[1] printed in all parts of Europe; though it has awakened the enthusiasm of thousands; though Mark Anthony Muret, one of the chief Catholic humanists of Campion's age, pronounced it to be "written by the finger of God," yet it is not an easy book for men of our generation to appreciate, and this precisely because it suited a bygone generation so exactly. Before it can be esteemed at its true value, some knowledge of the circumstances under which it was written, is indispensable.

§ 1. THE SIGNIFICANCE OF THE *Decem Rationes*.

The chief point to remember is that the *Decem Rationes* was the last and most deliberate free utterance of Campion's ever-memorable mission. During the few months that mission lasted he succeeded in staying the full tide of victorious Protestantism, which had hitherto been irresistible. The ancient Church had gone down before the new religion, at Elizabeth's accession twenty years be-

[1] Of these four are in English translations, dated 1606 (by Richard Stock), 1632, 1687, and 1827. The present translation is thus the fifth into Campion's mother tongue. Though each of the quaint old versions has its merits, and some do not lack charm, not one would adequately represent Campion to the modern reader. A new translation was a necessity—may I not say, a most happy one—seeing that Father Joseph Rickaby was at hand to satisfy it. [J.H.P.]

fore, with an apparently final fall, and since then the Elizabethan Settlement had triumphed in every church, in every school and court. The new generation had been moulded by it; the old order seemed to be utterly prostrate, defeated and moribund. Nor was it only at home that Protestantism talked of victory. In every neighbouring land she had gained or was gaining the upper hand. She had crossed the Border and subdued Scotland, she held Ireland in an iron grip, she had set up a new throne in Holland, she had deeply divided France, and had learned how to paralyze the power of Spain. What could stay her progress?

Then a new figure appeared, a fugitive flying before the law. He was hunted backwards and forwards across the country, every man's hand seemed against him. It was impossible to hold out for long against such immense odds, and he was in fact soon captured, mocked, maligned, sentenced and executed with contumely. Yet Campion and his handful of followers had meanwhile succeeded in doing what the whole nation, when united, had failed to do. He had evoked a spirit of faith and fervour, against which the violence of Protestantism raged in vain. He had saved the beaten, shattered fragments of the ancient host, and animated them with invincible courage; and his work endured in spite of endless assaults and centuries of persecution. The *Decem Rationes* is Campion's harangue to those whom he called upon to follow him in the heroic struggle.

§ 2. THE MAN AND THE MISSION.

Thus much for the inspiration and general significance of Campion's work considered as a whole. It will also repay a much more minute study, and to appreciate it we must enter into further details.

As to the man himself, suffice it to say that he was a Londoner; his father a publisher; his first school Christ's Hospital; that he was afterwards a Fellow of St. John's, Oxford, and held at the same time an exhibition from the Grocer's Company. At Oxford he accepted to some extent the Elizabethan Settlement of religion, but not sufficiently to satisfy the Company of Grocers, who eventually withdrew their exhibition. This was a sign for further inquisitorial proceedings, which made him leave the University, and retire to Dublin; but he was driven also thence by the zealots for Protestantism. Eventually he went over to the English College at Douay, whence he migrated to Rome, entered the Society of Jesus, and after eight years' training had returned, a priest, to his native country, forty years old. His strong point was undoubtedly a singularly lovable character, and he possessed the gift of eloquence in no ordinary degree. For the rest, his natural qualities and acquired accomplishments were above the ordinary level, without reaching an extraordinary height. He was a man who never ceased working, and whose temper was always angelic, though he sometimes suffered from severe depression. He was adored by his pupils both at Oxford and in Bohemia. His memory was always bright, and his conversation always sparkled with fresh thoughts and poetical ideas. He composed with extraordinary facility in Latin prose and verse; but the extant fragments of these literary exercises do not strike us as being of unusual excellence, though genuinely admired in their day. He was certainly an ideal missioner: saintly, inspired, eloquent, untireable, patient, consumed with the desire for the success of his undertaking, and unfaltering in his faith that success would follow by the providential action of God, despite the obvious fact that all appearances were against him.

Campion landed at Dover late in June, 1580, and reached London at the end of the month. There was an immediate rush to hear him, and Lord Paget was persuaded to lend his great hall at Paget House in Smithfield to accommodate a congregation for the feast of Saints Peter and Paul. The sermon was delivered on the text from the Gospel of the day, *Tu es Christus, Filius Dei vivi*. The hall was filled, and the impression caused by the sermon was profound; but the number of hearers had been imprudently large. Though no arrests followed, the persecutors took the alarm, and increased their activity to such an extent that large gatherings had for ever to be abandoned; and after a couple of weeks both Campion and Persons left London to escape the notice of the pursuivants, whose raids and inquisitorial searches were making the lot of Catholics in town unbearable, whereas in the country the pursuit was far less active, and could be much more easily avoided.

The two Fathers met for the last time at Hoxton, then a village outside London, to concert their plans for the next couple of months, and were on the point of starting, each for his own destination, when a Catholic of some note rode up from London. This was Thomas Pounde, of Belmont or Beaumont, near Bedhampton, a landed gentleman of means, an enthusiastic Catholic, and for the last five years or so a prisoner for religion. Mr. Pounde's message in effect was this. "You are going into the proximate danger of capture, and if captured you must expect not justice, but every refinement of misrepresentation. You will be asked crooked questions, and your answers to them will be published in some debased form. Be sure that whatever then comes through to the outer world will come out poisoned and perverted. Let me therefore urge you to write now, and to leave in safe custody, what you would wish to have published then, in case infamous rumours should be put about during your incarceration, rumours which you will then not be able to answer or to repudiate." Father Persons seems to have agreed at once. Campion at first raised objections, but soon, with his ever obliging temper, sat down at the end of the table and wrote off in half an hour an open letter *To the Lords of Her Majesty's Privy Council*, afterwards so well known as *Campion's Challenge*.

§ 3. THE CHALLENGE.

Campion, after finishing his letter and taking a copy for himself, had consigned the other copy to Pounde. Persons had done the same; but whereas the latter took the precaution to seal his letter, Campion had handed over his unfastened. Then the company broke up. Persons made a wide circle from Northampton round to Gloucester, while Campion made a smaller circle from Oxfordshire up to Northampton. When they got back to town in September, they found all the world discussing " the Challenge." What had happened was that proceedings had been taken by the Ecclesiastical Commission against Pounde, and he had been committed to solitary confinement in the ruinous castle of Bishop's Stortford. Before he left London he began to communicate the letter to others, lest it should be altogether lost, and as soon as it was thus published it attracted everyone's attention, and his adversaries had ironically christened it *the challenge*. The word was indeed one which Campion had used, but he had employed it precisely in order to avoid any charge that might have arisen, of being combative and presumptuous.

Thus in the course of three months Campion, as it were in spite of himself, had filled England with his name and with the message he had come to announce, and he had reduced his adversaries to a very ridiculous position. They had been dared to meet him in disputation, and this they feared to do. In effect, they in their thousands were hiding their heads in the sand, while their constables and pursuivants were raiding the houses of Catholics on every side in hopes of catching the homeless wanderer, and of stopping his mouth by violence. The pulpits, of course, rang with outcries against the newcomer, and in his absence his doctrines were rent and scoffed at; but, as Campion said in a contemporary letter, " The people hereupon is ours, and the error of spreading that letter abroad hath done us much good." This was the first popular success which the Catholics had scored for years; and after so many years of oppression some popular success was of immense importance to the cause. Father Persons, in a contemporary letter, says that the Government found that there were 50,000 more recusants that autumn than they had known of before. The number is, of course, a round one, and is possibly much exaggerated, but it gives the Catholic leader's view of the advantage won at this time.

We may now turn to *The Challenge* itself, the only piece of Campion's English during this his golden period, which has survived.

[TO THE RIGHT HONOURABLE, THE LORDS OF HER MAJESTIE'S PRIVY COUNCIL]

RIGHT HONOURABLE:

Whereas I have come out of Germanie and Boëmeland, being sent by my Superiors, and adventured myself into this noble Realm, my deare Countrie, for the glorie of God and benefit of souls, I thought it like enough that, in this busie watchful and suspicious worlde, I should either sooner or later be intercepted and stopped of my course. Wherefore, providing for all events, and uncertaine what may become of me, when God shall haply deliver my body into durance, I supposed it needful to put this writing in a readiness, desiringe your good Lordships to give it ye reading, for to know my cause.

This doing I trust I shall ease you of some labour. For that which otherwise you must have sought for by practice of wit, I do now lay into your hands by plaine confession. And to ye intent that the whole matter may be conceived in order, and so the better both understood and remembered, I make thereof these ix points or articles, directly, truly and resolutely opening my full enterprise and purpose.

i. I confesse that I am (albeit unworthie) a priest of ye Catholike Church, and through ye great mercie of God vowed now these viii years into the Religion of the Societie of Jhesus. Hereby I have taken upon me a special kind of warfare under the banner of obedience, and eke resigned all my interest or possibilitie of wealth, honour, pleasure, and other worldlie felicitie.

ii. At the voice of our General Provost, which is to me a warrant from heaven, and Oracle of Christ, I tooke my voyage from Prage to Rome (where our said General Father is always resident) and from Rome to England, as I might and would have done joyously into any part of Christendome or Heathenesse, had I been thereto assigned.

iii. My charge is, of free cost to preach the Gospel, to minister the Sacraments, to instruct the simple, to reforme sinners, to confute errors—in brief, to crie alarme spiritual against foul vice and proud ignorance, wherewith many my dear Countrymen are abused.

iv. I never had mind, and am strictly forbidden by our Father that sent me, to deal in any respect with matter of State or Policy of this realm, as things which appertain not to my vocation, and from which I do gladly restrain and sequester my thoughts.

v. I do ask, to the glory of God, with all humility, and under your correction, iii sortes of indifferent and quiet audiences: *the first* before your Honours, wherein I will discourse of religion, so far as it toucheth the common weale and your nobilities: *the second*, whereof I make more account, before the Doctors and Masters and chosen men of both Universities, wherein I undertake to avow the faith of our Catholike Church by proofs innumerable, Scriptures, Councils, Fathers, History, natural and moral reasons: *the third* before the lawyers, spiritual and temporal, wherein I will justify the said faith by the common wisdom of the laws standing yet in force and practice.

vi. I would be loth to speak anything that might sound of any insolent brag or challenge, especially being now as a dead man to this world and willing to put my head under every man's foot, and to kiss the ground they tread upon. Yet have I such a courage in avouching the Majesty of Jhesus my King, and such affiance in his gracious favour, and such assurance in my quarrel, and my evidence so impregnable, and because I know perfectly that no one Protestant, nor all the Protestants living, nor any sect of our adversaries (howsoever they face men down in pulpits, and overrule us in their kingdom of grammarians and unlearned ears)[1] can maintain their doctrine in disputation. (I am to sue most humbly and instantly for the combat with all and every of them, and the most principal that may be found: protesting that in this trial the better furnished they come, the better welcome they shall be.)

vii. And because it hath pleased God to enrich the Queen my Sovereign Ladye with notable gifts of nature, learning, and princely education, I do verily trust that—if her Highness would vouchsafe her royal person and good attention to such a conference as, in the ii part of my fifth article I have motioned, or to a few sermons, which in her or your hearing I am

---

[1] The meaning is—" The ministers tyrannize over us, as if we were a kingdom of unlearned schoolboys listening to a teacher of grammar."

to utter,—such manifest and fair light by good method and plain dealing may be cast upon these controversies, that possibly her zeal of truth and love of her people shall incline her noble Grace to disfavour some proceedings hurtful to the Realm, and procure towards us oppressed more equitie.

viii. Moreover I doubt not but you her Highness' Council being of such wisdom and discreet in cases most important, when you shall have heard these questions of religion opened faithfully, which many times by our adversaries are huddled up and confounded, will see upon what substantial grounds our Catholike Faith is builded, how feeble that side is which by sway of the time prevaileth against us, and so at last for your own souls, and for many thousand souls that depend upon your government, will discountenance error when it is bewrayed, and hearken to those who would spend the best blood in their bodies for your salvation. Many innocent hands are lifted up to heaven for you daily by those English students, whose posteritie shall never die, which beyond seas gathering virtue and sufficient knowledge for the purpose, are determined never to give you over, but either to win you heaven, or to die upon your pikes. And touching our Societie be it known to you that we have made a league—all the Jesuits in the world, whose succession and multitude must overreach all the practices of England—cheerfully to carry the cross you shall lay upon us, and never to despair your recovery, while we have a man left to enjoy your Tyburn, or to be racked with your torments, or consumed with your prisons. The expense is reckoned, the enterprise is begun; it is of God, it cannot be withstood. So the faith was planted: so it must be restored.

ix. If these my offers be refused, and my endeavours can take no place, and I, having run thousands of miles to do you good, shall be rewarded with rigour, I have no more to say but to recommend your case and mine to Almightie God, the Searcher of Hearts, who send us His grace, and set us at accord before the day of payment, to the end we may at last be friends in heaven, when all injuries shall be forgotten.

"Direct, true, and resolute," Campion's words certainly are, and they are calculated in a remarkable degree to reassure and animate his fellow Catholics and their friends, and it is for them in reality, rather than for the Lords of the Council, that the message is composed. If the composition has a fault it is its combativeness; and in effect, though this drawback was not felt at the time, it was later. Subsequent missionaries found it best to adopt a policy of far greater secrecy and silence. If, however, we remember that Campion intended his paper to be published under quite different circumstances, we can see that he at least hardly deserves the reproach of being contentious, or if he does, his failing was venial when we consider the tastes of the age. The immediate result of the publication was without question a great success.

§ 4. THE "DECEM RATIONES."

Like a wise general, Father Persons at once bethought himself how best to follow up the good beginning already made. Accordingly, when he and Campion met at Uxbridge (for it was not safe for Campion to come to London), he suggested that the latter, seeing that his memory was still green at Oxford, should compose a short address on the crisis to the students of the two Universities. Campion met the suggestion as he had met the suggestion of Pounde, with a gentle disclaimer, "alleging divers difficulties," but soon good-humouredly assented on the condition (not a usual one with literary men) that someone else should propose the subject. The company therefore made various suggestions, none of which met with general acceptance, until Campion proposed "Heresy in Despair." "Whereat," adds Persons, "all that were present could not choose but laugh, and wonder to see him fall upon that argument at such a time when heresy seemed most of all to triumph." In truth, with England invincible at sea and on land, and the absolute sway of Elizabeth, Cecil, and Walsingham over both Church and State, what more hopeful position for Protestantism could have been imagined? Campion's meaning, of course, was that Protestantism was in despair of holding the position of the ancient Church; of ruling in the hearts of a free people; of co-existing with Christian liberty. It was unworthy, therefore, of the acceptance of minds that aspired to mental freedom, as did the youth of the Universities. This subject for an address was welcomed with acclamation, and Campion promised to undertake it, suggesting on his side that Persons should arrange ways and means for printing the tract when finished, and any other which might seem needed.

This agreed to, all separated once more, and Campion rode northwards on a tour which he took in

Derbyshire, Yorkshire, and Lancashire, and which was not over for six months. Meantime Father Persons had set up his " magic press " near London, and issued from it five volumes of small size indeed, but of remarkable vigour and merit. As soon as any notable attack was made on the Catholics, an answer was brought out in a wonderfully short time, and these answers were pithy, vigorous, and pointed, in no ordinary degree. When one remembers how much co-operation is needed to bring out even the slightest volume, one is truly astonished at the feat of bringing out so many and such good ones, while the hourly fear of capture, torture, and death hung over the heads of all. When threatened with danger in one place the press was bodily transported to another.

However, our business at present is not with Persons, but with Campion. His book was finished and sent up to Persons in March, 1581, with a title altered to suit the controversy which had already begun. It was now *Decem Rationes: quibus fretus, certamen adversariis obtulit in causa Fidei, Edmundus Campianus &c.* " Ten Reasons, for the confidence with which Edmund Campion offered his adversaries to dispute on behalf of the Faith, set before the famous men of our Universities." Persons was charmed, as he had expected to be, with its literary grace. It was in Latin, as had been agreed, and Campion's Latin prose, (though critics of our time find it somewhat silvery and Livian), suited the tastes of that day to perfection. The only thing which made Persons at all thoughtful was the number of references. Campion declared that he was sure he had verified them, as he entered them in his notebook, but Persons, with greater caution, declared that they must be verified anew.

The difficulty of this for men living under the ban, and cut off from access to large libraries, was of course great, but through the help of others, especially through Mr. Thomas Fitzherbert of Swynnerton, the task was happily accomplished. Campion came up from the north to Stonor, on the Oxfordshire border where the secret press then was; and there, amid a thousand fears, alarms and dangers, the book was printed.

§ 5. THE PRINTING.

Of the actual preparations for printing the *Ten Reasons*, Persons gives this account in his Memoirs[1]:

Persons was of opinion that Campion should come up to London immediately after Easter [March 26th] to examine the passages quoted, and to assist the print. Meanwhile Persons began to prepare new means of printing, making use of friends and in particular of a certain priest called William Morris, a learned and resourceful man, who afterwards died in Rome.[2] This was necessary, as the first press near London, where the first two books had been printed, had been taken down. Eventually and with very great difficulty he found, after much trying, a house belonging

---

[1] *Catholic Record Society* IV., 14-17.
[2] Father Bombino calls him Richard Morris, and says he went into exile and lived with Allen first at Rheims, and afterwards at Rome, where he died in the English College. (*Vita Campiani*, p. 139).

to a widow, by name Lady Stonor, in which she was not living at that time. It was situated in the middle of a wood, twenty miles from London.

To this house were taken all things necessary, that is, type, press, paper, &c., though not without many risks. Mr. Stephen Brinkley, a gentleman of high attainments both in literature and in virtue, superintended the printing. Father Campion then coming to London, with his book already revised, went at once to the house in the wood, where the book was printed and eventually published. Persons too went down to stay with him for some days to take counsel on their affairs.

Stonor Park, to which Campion and Persons had betaken themselves,[1] is still in the possession of the old Catholic family of that name, of which Lord Camoys is the representative. Father Morris says that " the printing, according to the traditions of the place, was carried on in the attics of the old house."[2] Being near Henley it was possible to go there by road or by water, and one might come and go on the Oxford high-road without attracting attention.

Still there was grave risk of discovery from the noise made by the press, and from the number of extra men about the house, as to the fidelity of each of whom it was impossible to be absolutely

[1] Father Morris identified the lady who let or lent Stonor Park, with Dame Cecilia Stonor, daughter of Leonard Chamberlain. Father Persons describes her as a widow, and if so, the Sir Francis, then alive, was not her husband, but her son. Both father and son had the same Christian name.

[2] On the other hand, Mr. Thomas Edward Stonor, in a correspondence to be mentioned immediately, says that there were no definite traditions as to the actual locality of the press.

sure. Day by day the dangers thickened round them. One evening, soon after their arrival, William Hartley, a priest and afterwards a martyr, who was helping in the work, and had then just come back from a visit to Oxford, mentioned casually that Roland Jenks, the Catholic stationer and bookbinder there, was again in trouble, having been accused by his own servant. Jenks was doubtless known to all Oxford men, indeed but three years before his name had been noised all over Europe. He had been sentenced to have his ears cut off for some religious offence, when the Judge was taken ill in the court itself, and, the infection travelling with marvellous rapidity, the greater part both of the bench and of the jury were stricken down with gaol fever, and two judges, twelve justices, and other high officials, almost the whole jury, and many others, died within the space of two days.[1]

In mentioning Jenks's new troubles Hartley probably did not realize the extent of the danger to the whole party which they portended. Persons had in fact employed the very servant who had now turned traitor, to bind a number of books for him at his house near Bridewell Church, London, which with all its contents was thus in a perilous condition. Early next morning an express messenger was sent in to town with orders to hide or destroy Persons' papers and other effects. It was already too late: that very night the house had been searched, and Persons' letters, books, vestments, rosaries, pictures, and other pious objects,

[1] Challoner, *Missionary Priests*, Introd. p. 12.

had all fallen into the hands of the pursuivants. Worse still, Father Alexander Briant, afterwards a martyr, and one of the brightest and most lovable of the missionaries, was seized next door, and hurried off first to the Counter, then to the Tower, where he was repeatedly and most cruelly racked to make him say where Persons might be found.

Information about his torture was brought to the Jesuits at Stonor, and one can easily see how grave and disturbing such bad news must have been. "For almost the whole of one night," says Persons, "Campion and I sat up talking of what we had better do, if we should fall into their hands. A fate which befell him soon after."

The Registers of the Privy Council inform us that their Lordships gave orders to have Jenks sent up to London on the 28th of April. This settles approximately the date of the beginning of the printing at Stonor, and the book was not finished till nearly the end of June. So the work lasted about nine weeks, a fairly long period when we consider the smallness of the Latin book, here reproduced. It will, however, be shown from intrinsic evidence, that the stock of type was very small. The printers had to set up a few pages at a time, to correct them at once, and to print off, before they could go any further. Then they distributed the type, and began again. When all was finished they rapidly stabbed and bound their sheets. Considering the fewness of the workmen[1] and the un-

[1] As five printers were subsequently arrested, we know their names, and they deserve to be recorded here, viz., Stephen Brinkley, John Harris, John Hervey, John Tuker, John Compton. Allen speaks of seven workmen. *Diary of the Tower* and *Douay Diary*.

C

foreseen delays which so often occur during printing, the time taken over the production does not seem extraordinary.

For many years no example of the original edition of the *Decem Rationes* was known to exist: none of our great public libraries in London or at the Universities possesses a copy. But it was the singular good fortune of the late Marquess of Bute to pick up two copies of this extremely rare volume, and he munificently presented one of them to Stonyhurst College. Canon Gunning of Winchester is the happy owner of a third copy. By the courtesy of the Rector of Stonyhurst, I am able to offer a minute description of the precious little book.

The volume is, considering the printing of that time, distinctly well got up. There is nothing at first sight to suggest that its publication had been a matter of so much difficulty and danger; but when one scrutinizes every page with care, one finds that it bears about it some traces of the unusual circumstances under which it was produced.

If we look first for the water-mark in the paper we shall find that it is the pot—the ordinary English sign; a proof, if one were needed, that the book was really printed in this country. The sheets run from A to K (with prefixed ‡), in fours, 16mo; the folios are 44, of which 39 are numbered (but by accident the pagination is omitted from 1 to 4, and 40 is blank as well as the fly-leaves).

Let us think of what this means. Eleven signatures for 44 folios, 16mo, means that only eight pages 16mo went into each printing frame, or, in other words, that the frame was so small that it would have been covered by half a folio sheet, 9 by 13 inches. They probably printed off each little sheet by itself, for if they had had a larger frame so as to print an entire folio sheet—then we should have found in the finished book that the watermark would recur once in each sixteen pages. In point of fact, however, it only recurs irregularly in the first, fifth, and tenth gathering. This could not have occurred unless the sheets used were of half folio size.

A Greek fount was evidently wanting. Campion was fond, after the fashion of scholars of that day, of throwing into his Latin letters a word or two of Greek, which in his autograph are written, as Mr. Simpson has remarked, with the facility of one familiar with the language. Here on fol. 24 a we find *adynata*, where ἀδύνατα would have been in Campion's epistolary manner. Again, on fol. 4 b he quotes, " Hic calix novum testamentum in sanguine meo, qui (calix) pro vobis fundetur," and in the margin *Poterion Ekchynomenon*, in Italics, where Greek script, if obtainable, would obviously have been preferred. A further indication of the difficulties under which type had been procured is seen in the use of a query sign of a black-letter fount (*i.e.*, ?) instead of the Roman fount *i.e.*, ?). This will be the more readily comprehended when we remember that Father Persons' books, which Brinkley had printed before, were in English, and that English prose was then still generally printed in Gothic character.[1]

So Persons also made use of it in order that there might be nothing in his books to strike the eye as unusual in books of that class. Campion's volume on the other hand being in Latin, it was necessary to procure a new set of " Roman " type. The use of the black-letter query-signs would not at once attract attention, so they were kept, though all else was changed.

A further trace of the difficulty in finding type is found in the signs for *a, e*, diphthong.

This combination recurred very frequently in Latin, and the printers had very few of them. Very soon after starting we find them substituting for Roman an Italic diphthong, æ, also o, e (œ), and even e, an ordinary mediæval form of the sign. It will be noticed that these substitutions become increasingly frequent, as we approach fol. 12 (end of signature C), fol. 32 (end of signature H), and 36 (end of signature I), whereas as soon as the next signature begins the fount of æ is ready to hand again. The conclusion to be deduced is that leaves C, H, and I were each printed off, and the type distributed, before the setting up of D, I, and K could be proceeded with. This illustrates what has been said before of the very small stock of type in the printing establishment.

Another slight peculiarity ought perhaps to be

[1] The custom however was already changing, and " Roman " type soon afterwards came into general use.

noticed: it is the accentuation of the Latin. Adverbs, for instance, are generally accented on the last syllable, *e.g.*, *doctiùs, facilè, quám, eó, quó:* the rule, however, is by no means regularly kept. But this has evidently nothing to do with the peculiar conditions under which Campion's book was produced, and is to be accounted for by the use of accents in other publications of the same class. Nothing was then definitely settled about the accentuation of either French, Italian, or Latin, and Campion's volume does but reproduce the uncertainty on the matter which was everywhere prevalent.

Whilst the printers were contending with the difficulties arising from the smallness of their stock of type, difficulties which no doubt caused vexatious and dangerous delays, Campion and Persons resumed their missionary labours with vigour. In his *Memoirs* Persons writes:

Whilst the preparations were being made Campion preached unweariedly, sometimes in London, sometimes making excursions. There was one place [that of the Bellamy's] whither we often went, about five miles from London, called Harohill. In going thither we had to pass through Tyburn. But Campion would always pass bareheaded, and making a deep bow, both because of the sign of the Cross, and in honour of some martyrs who had suffered there, and also because he used to say that he would have his combat there.[1]

[1] *Memoirs*, i. cap. 24; *Collectanea P.* fol. 155.

Father Bombino[1] managed to find out some further details. Mrs. Bellamy's house, he tells us, had a good library, and as to Campion's conduct at Tyburn, he explains that the shape of the gallows was a triangle, supported at its three angles by three baulks of timber; the tie-beams, however, suggested to Campion the Cross of Christ.

From the State Papers we hear of other families and places said to have been visited by Campion at this period: the Prices, of Huntingdon; Mr. William Griffith, of Uxbridge; Mr. Edwin East, of Bledlow, Bucks; Lady Babington, at Twyford, Bucks; Mr. Dormer, at Wynge, and Mrs. Pollard.[2]

In spite of alarms, dangers, and interruptions, the work of printing was concluded without mishap. The method of publication was singular.

---

[1] Bombino, *Vita Campiani* 1620, p. 136. Some of Bombino's additions are not, perhaps, arranged in their true chronological order. He tells us, for instance, *à propos* of Brinkley's difficulties in getting printers, that he had to dress them, and give them horses to ride, like gentlemen. But he does not make it clear whether these were the men who printed the *Ten Reasons*, or Persons' previous works. Bombino says that Brinkley paid for the type, &c., but Allen, in a contemporary letter, says that George Gilbert had left a fund for these purposes. Bombino says the printing of the *Decem Rationes* was commenced at Brinkley's own house at Green Street, and had to be removed because one of the servants was arrested in London, and tortured to make him confess, which he heroically refused. Campion and Persons knowing of the torture, not of the man's constancy, at once removed the press. But Persons' *Memoirs* ascribes this incident to an earlier period. (*Domestical Difficulties*, p. 119; *Autobiography* for 1581).

[2] Simpson, p. 217, following Lansdowne MSS. xxx. 78.

Hartley took the bulk of the copies to Oxford, where the chief academical display of the year, the Act, as it was called, was taking place in St. Mary's, on several successive days. Hartley, coming in at the end of the first day, waited for every one to go out, then slipped his little books under the papers left on the seats, and was gone. Next morning he entered with the rest, and soon saw that his plan had been perfectly successful. The public disputation began, but the attention of the audience was elsewhere. There was whispering and comparing notes, and passing about of little books, and as soon as the séance was over, open discussion of Campion's "Reasons." Hartley did not wait for more, but rode back to Stonor with the news that the book had surely hit its mark.

At Oxford, as Father Persons says, many remembered and loved the man, or at least knew of his gentle character, and of the career he had abandoned to become a Catholic missionary. The book recalled all this; and to those who were able to enter into its spirit it preached with a strange penetrating force. By all the lovers of classical Latin, and there were many such at that day, it was read greedily. The Catholics and lovers of the old Faith received it with enthusiasm, but a still more valid testimony to its power was given by the Protestant Government, which gave orders to its placemen that they should elaborate replies. These replies drew forth answers from the Catholics, and the controversy lasted for several years. Mr. Simpson has included an outline of this controversy in his *Life of Campion,* and to it I may refer my readers, having nothing substantial to add to his account.

§ 6. CRITICISM.

It would not be necessary for me to say more about its success, except that to us nowadays, the *Rationes* will not seem at all so remarkable as it did to our ancestors. Religious controversy, in itself, does not much interest us moderns; and those who will read Latin merely to enjoy the style are very few. But in the sixteenth century, as Sir Arthur Helps truly says, men found in the thrill of controversy the interest they now take in novels. At that time, too, of all literary charms, that of good Latin prose was by far the most popular, and the language was still the " lingua franca " of the learned all the world over. Once we get so far as to appreciate that both subject and style were in its favour, the popularity of the volume will seem natural enough, for it is bright, pointed, strong, full of matter, bold, eloquent, convincing.

Without attempting anything like a complete account of the reception of the book by the public, I may mention as the most obvious proof of its popularity, that more strenuous endeavours were made (so far as I can discover) to answer it than were made in the case of any other assault upon the Elizabethan religious settlement. Lord Burghley himself, the chief minister of the Crown, called upon the Bishop of London, perhaps the most forward man then on the episcopal bench, to use all endeavours to ensure the publication of a sufficent answer. Finally they appointed the Regius Professors of Divinity both at Oxford and at Cambridge to provide for the occasion, and it took both of these a long series of months to propound their answers to Campion's tract, which is only as long as a magazine article. Speaking broadly, we may say that this was the most that Elizabeth's Establishment could do officially; and besides this, there were sermons innumerable, and pamphlets not a few by lesser men, as well as disputations in the Tower, of which more must be said later.

This hostile evidence is so striking and so ample that it might seem unnecessary to allege more, but I attach a great deal more importance to the praise of theologians of Campion's own faith: for, in the first place this is much harder to obtain than the attention of the persons attacked. Secondly, those who are acquainted with Catholic theological criticism are at first surprised to find what very severe critics Catholic theologians are one of another. In this case, where the writer had from the nature of his task to make so much use of rhetorical arguments, allusions, irony, and unusual forms of expression, there was more than usual chance of fault being found, especially as every possible thorny subject is introduced somehow, and that in terms meant to please not Roman theologians, but Oxford students. Evidently there was danger here that critics should or might be severe, or at least insist on certain changes and emendations. In fact the work was received with joy, and reprinted frequently and with honour. I have lately found a letter in its commendation from the Cardinal Secretary of State of that day, and Muret, as we have heard, perhaps the greatest humanist then living in the Catholic ranks, described it as " Libellum aureum, vere digito Dei scriptum."

§ 7. THE DISPUTATIONS.

The publication of the *Decem Rationes* was the last act of Campion's life of freedom. He was seized the very next week, and after five months of suffering was martyred on 1 December, 1581. During that prolonged and unequal struggle against every variety of craft and violence the *Ten Reasons* continued to have their influence, and on the whole they were extremely helpful, for they enabled the martyr to recover some ground which he had lost while under torture. During those awful agonies he confessed to having found shelter in the houses of certain gentlemen. It is certain that these names were all known to the Government before, and that he was not betraying any secret. Nevertheless the gentlemen in question were at once seized, imprisoned and fined, on the alleged evidence of Campion's confessions only. This of course caused much scandal among Catholics, and so long as he lay lost in the Tower dungeons, unpleasant rumours about his constancy could not be effectively contradicted. Thus far Elizabeth's ministers had gained an advantage, which Pounde had foretold they were likely to win. But the remedy he had suggested also proved effective.

Though under ordinary circumstances Elizabeth's ministers "meant nothing less" than having the disputation requested, nevertheless now that Campion was so terribly shaken and reduced, they hoped that they might arrange some sort of a meeting, which might in show correspond with what had been demanded in the *Decem Rationes*, and yet leave them with a certain victory. They were emboldened too, by finding that their prisoner was not after all, such a particularly learned man. He had never been a professor of theology, or written or made special studies, beyond the ordinary course which in those days was not a long one. It was, therefore, settled that four disputations should be held in the Tower of London. Theology was still taught at Oxford and Cambridge in something of the old mediæval method and in syllogistic form. The men who were pitted against Campion had lately been, or were still, examiners at the Universities. Nor is it to be denied for a moment that they did their work well. The attack never faltered. Their own side quite believed they had won. The method they adopted was this. They assumed the rôle of examiners, and starting with the *Decem Rationes* before them, they plied Campion with crabbed texts, and obscure quotations from the Fathers. Then they cut short his answers, and as soon as one had examined for one quarter of an hour, another took his place, for they were anxious above all things to avoid defeat. The number of topics broached and left unsettled surpasses belief, indeed the scene was one of utter confusion, taunts, scoldings, sneers—a very, very different test from the academic argumentation, which Campion had requested.

The martyr did not show any remarkable erudition, indeed all opportunity to do so was carefully shut off. No University, I fancy, would have given him a chair of theology on the strength of his replies on that occasion. There was more than one premature assertion of victory on the Protestant side. But when the Catholic and Protestant accounts are compared, one sees that the advantages won against Campion were slight. They evidently hoped that by vigorous and repeated attacks they would at last puzzle or bear him down. But they were never near this. He was always fresh and gay, never in difficulties, or at the end of his tether. He stands out quite the noblest, the most sympathetic and important figure in those motley assemblies. The Catholics were delighted. They succeeded in getting their own report of the disputations, which is still extant, and they would have printed it, if they had been able. Philip, Earl of Arundel, by far the most important convert of that generation, was won over by what he heard in those debates.

On the whole then we must say that, if Campion did not come off gloriously, he at least acquitted himself well and honourably, and distinctly gained by the conflict. Offers of disputation were not the ideal way of forwarding a mission such as his. Nevertheless, in his case, despite circumstances the most adverse, the result had proved advantageous.

It had greatly strengthened and encouraged his own followers, and that was in reality the best that could then be expected. Incidentally too the adverse rumours, which had gained ground during his seclusion, were dissipated. It was clear that, though he might have been deceived, his constancy was unconquerable.

Thus Campion's *Challenge* and his *Ten Reasons* not only contain the message of his mission enunciated with characteristic eloquence, but the delivery of each message is an history-making event, big with dramatic consequences. The controversy about his book did not die with him, but continued for some years, until it was merged into the standing controversy between the two religions. We cannot describe it here.

Suffice it to say that Mr. Simpson, in the *Appendix* to his *Edmund Campion* enumerates not less than twenty works, which appeared in those controversies between 1581 and 1585. The chief defender of Father Campion's writings was Father Robert Drury, S.J., but all his biographers also have something to say on the subject. The chief opponents are William Charke, Meredith Hanmer, William Fulke, Laurence Humphrey, William Whitaker, R. Stoke, John Field, Alexander Nowell, and William Day. Some further information on the whole subject may be found in articles by the late Father Morris and myself in *The Month* for July 1889, January 1905, and January 1910.

J.H.P.

RATIONES DECEM

QVIBVS FRETVS B. EDMVNDVS CAMPIANVS CERTAMEN ADVERSARIIS OBTVLIT IN CAVSA FIDEI, REDDITAE ACADEMICIS ANGLIAE.

EPISTOLA[1]

AD REGINAE ANGLIAE CONSILIARIOS, QUA PROFECTIONIS SUAE IN ANGLIAM INSTITUTUM DECLARAT, ET ADVERSARIOS AD CERTAMEN PROVOCAT

Quandoquidem, viri ornatissimi, a Germania et Bohemia revocatus, non sine ingenti vitae meae periculo, in hoc florentissimum Angliae regnum, dulcissimam patriam meam, tandem aliquando perveni, pro Superiorum meorum voluntate, Dei gloriam et animarum salutem promoturus; verisimile esse putavi, me turbulento hoc, suspicioso ac difficillimo tempore, sive citius, sive aliquanto tardius, in medio cursu abreptum iri. Quapropter ignarus quid de me futurum sit, quum Dei permissu in carceres et vincula forte detrudendus sim, ad omnem eventum scriptum hoc condidi: quod ut legere, et ex eo causam meam cognoscere velitis, etiam atque etiam rogo. Fiet enim, ut hac re non parvo labore liberemini, dum quod multis ambagibus inquirere vos audio, id totum aperta confessione libere expromo. Atque ut rem omnem, quo

---

[1] A Beato Edmundo anglice scripta, ab alio latine reddita.

melius et intelligi, et memoria comprehendi queat, compendio tradam, in novem omnino capita eam dispertiar.

1. Profiteor me, quamvis indignum, Ecclesiae Catholicae sacerdotem, et iam octo abhinc annis magna Dei misericordia in Societatem nominis Iesu cooptatum, peculiare quoddam belli genus sub obedientiae vexillo suscepisse; ac simul me omni divitiarum, honorum et aliorum huiusmodi bonorum spe, et habendi potestate, abdicasse.

2. Generalis Praepositi nostri decreto (quod ego tamquam mandatum coelitus missum, et a Christo ipso sancitum veneror), Praga Romam, ubi Generalis nostri perpetua sedes est; Roma deinde in Angliam contendi: qua animi alacritate etiam in quamcumque aliam orbis terrarum partem, sive ad christianos, sive ad infideles, profectus fuissem, si me ad eam profectionem superiores mei designassent.

3. Negotium mihi commisum tale est, ut gratis Evangelium administrem, rudes in fide instituam, flagitiosos a scelere ad meliorem vitae rationem traducam, errores convellam; et, ut summatim omnia complectar, pugnae spiritualis signum tuba canam, atque alacriter adversus foeda flagitia et superbam ignorationem, qua innumeri cives mei, quos intimis animi visceribus complector, oppressi iacent, depugnem.

4. Numquam mihi animus fuit, imo et a Patribus, qui me miserunt, severe prohibitum mihi est, ut ne reipublicae ac politicae huius regni administrationis negotiis me immisceam: nam et

aliena haec sunt a vocationis meae instituto, et iis animum cogitationesque meas libenter avoco.

5. Quamobrem vestra clementia fretus, ad gloriam Dei tria non minus aequa, quam ab omni pacis et tranquillitatis reipublicae perturbatione aliena, concedi mihi et permitti humillime postulo. Primum est, ut Dominationes vestrae, pro sua et reipublicae dignitate, me pro religione disserentem audire non graventur. Alterum, quod et cumprimis desidero, et maximi momenti esse arbitror, ut mihi liceat in consessu doctorum, magistorum et utriusque Academiae virorum insignium, sacrosanctae theologiae professorum, verba facere. Promitto me catholicae Ecclesiae fidem invictis rationibus et sacrarum Scripturarum, Conciliorum, Patrum atque historiarum auctoritate, ac denique ex ipsa tum naturali, tum morali philosophia efficaciter demonstraturum et defensurum. Tertium, ut audiar ab utriusque iuris, sive canonici, sive civilis, peritis, quibus eamdem fidei veritatem, legum, quae etiamnum vigent, testimonio atque auctoritate comprobabo.

6. Nollem equidem quidquam proferre, quod insolentem provocationem aut arrogantiam aliquam prae se ferret; quum et mundo mortuus iam sim, et ex animo paratus promtusque, ut me ad cuiusvis pedes abiiciam ac vestigia etiam exosculer. Tantus tamen animus mihi est pro gloria et maiestate Regis mei Iesu amplificanda, tanta in eius favore fiducia, tanta denique in causae aequitate et firmissimorum argumentorum ac probationum robore confidentia, (quum certo sciam nullum protestantium, nec om-

nes simul iunctos, nec ullam adversariorum factionem, quantumvis imperitam multitudinem et grammaticos quosdam adolescentulos, apud quos insigniter debacchantur, in errorem inducant, posse dogmata sua disputatione aut tueri aut probare); ut cum illis omnibus, vel cum eorum quolibet, vel cum antesignanis ex omni illorum numero delectis, ultro me offeram congressurum; bona fide protestans eo mihi gratius fore certamen, quo melius instructi accesserint.

7. Et quoniam Dominus Deus Dominam meam reginam, eximiis naturae, eruditionis ac regiae educationis dotibus exornare voluit, si sua Maiestas huiusmodi auditionem, qualem in quinto articulo secundo loco efflagitavi, sua regali praesentia et benigna attentione cohonestare dignaretur, sperarem sane, me articulos controversos optima methodo et perspicuis argumentis ita illustrare, atque ab omnibus fallaciarum involucris quibus constricti sunt, explicare posse, ut zelo veritatis et amore, quo sua Maiestas populum complectitur, mediocriter eius animum inclinarem, quum ad plurimas res, quae regno suo non parum detrimenti afferunt, damnandas et reiiciendas, tum ad nos catholicos, misere iamdiu oppressos, maiore aequitate prosequendos.

8. Neque vero dubium mihi est quin vos, ornatissimi consiliari S. M., quum in maximi momenti negotiis praeclare ac sapienter agere soleatis, ubi has de fide controversias, quas adversarii nostri non sine fuco et confuse plerumque pertractant, bona fide delectas et fuco nudatas perspexeritis, luce meridiana clarius cognituri sitis, quam solidis et

firmis fundamentis fides catholica nitatur. Et quia e contrario protestantium argumenta sunt omnino frivola et infirma, quae temporis iniquitate vim aliquam contra nos habere putantur; futurum spero, ut vestrarum animarum et innumerabilium aliarum, quae a vestro nutu et exemplo pendent, miserti, ab huiusmodi falsorum dogmatum architectis et doctoribus facies vestras animumque ipsum avertatis, ac nobis, qui vitam nostram pro vestra salute alacriter profundere parati sumus, aequiori et magis propitia mente auscultetis. Multae innocentes manus quotidie et sine intermissione pro vobis in coelum attolluntur. Haec in vos studia sunt eorum Anglorum, qui in provinciis transmarinis numquam interiturae posteritatis patres, virtuti et eruditioni adquirendae dant operam; omninoque secum statuerunt, a salute vestra promovenda non prius absistere, quam vel animas vestras Christo lucrifecerint, vel lanceis vestras confixi generose occubuerint. Et quidem quod ad Societatem nostram attinet, velim sciatis, omnes nos, qui sumus de Societate Iesu, per totum terrarum orbem longe lateque diffusi, (quorum continua successio et multitudo omnes machinationes vestras anglicas facile superabit), sanctum foedus iniisse ut cruces, quas nobis iniicietis, magno animo feramus, neque unıquam de vestra salute desperemus, quamdiu vel unus quispiam e nobis supererit, qui Tiburno[1] vestro fruatur, atque suppliciis vestris excarnificari, carceribusque squalere et consumi possit. Iampridem inita ratio est, divinique numinis auspicio incho-

[1] Est hic locus supplicii anglice *Tyburn*.

atum certamen; nulla vis, nullus impetus adversariorum superabit. Hac ratione consita et tradita olim fides est, eadem in pristinam dignitatem revocari et restitui debet.

Quod si hoc scriptum meum, quod offero, reiicitur, nec benevoli conatus mei quidquam possint efficere, et pro itinere multorum millium milliarium vestri causa suscepto, ingratum animum experiar; id unum agendum mihi supererit, ut vos causamque meam Deo scrutatori cordium commendem: quem quidem ex animo precor, ut nobis tantisper gratiam suam impertiri velit, qua ante extremum remunerationis diem in unam sententiam conspiremus; et ut tandem aliquando in coelo, ubi nulla erit iniuriarum memoria, amicitia sempiterna perfruamur.

PREFATIO

EDMVNDVS CAMPIANVS DOCTISSIMIS ACADEMICIS OXONII FLORENTIBVS ET CANTABRIGIAE, S. P. D.

Anno praeterito, quum ex instituto vitae meae iussus in hanc insulam remeassem, clarissimi viri, offendi sane fluctus haud paulo saeviores in anglicano littore, quam quos in oceano brittannico recens a tergo reliqueram. Mox interiorem in Angliam ubi penetrassem, nihil familiarius, quam inusitata supplicia; nihil certius, quam incerta pericula. Collegi me, ut potui, memor causae, memor temporum. Ac ne prius forte corriperer, quam auditus a quopiam fuissem, scripto protinus mandavi consilium meum, qui venissem, quid quaererem, quod bellum, et quibus, indicere cogitarem Autographum

apud me habui, ut mecum, si caperer, caperetur;
exemplum eius apud amicum deposui, quod, me
quidem nesciente, pluribus communicatum est. Adversarii publicatam schedulam atrociter acceperunt
quum caetera, tum illud invidiosissime criminantes,
quod unus omnibus in hoc religionis negotio certamen obtulissem; quamquam solus non eram futurus, si fide publica disputassem. Responderunt
postulatis meis Hammerus et Charcus. Quid tandem? Otiose omnia. Nullum enim responsum,
praeter unum, honeste dabunt, quod numquam dabunt: " Conditiones amplectimur, Regina spondet,
advola." Interea clamant isti: " Sodalitium tuum,
seditiones tuas, arrogantiam tuam, proditorem, sine
dubio proditorem." Ridicule. Operam et oleum
et famam homines non insipientissimi cur profundunt?

Verum his duobus, (quorum prior animi causa
meam chartam delegit, in quam incurrerat; alter
malitiosius totam rem convolvit), praebitus nuper
est libellus admodum luculentus, qui quantum oportuit, tantum et de Societate nostra, et de horum
iniuriis, et de provincia, quam sustinemus, edisserit.
Mihi supererat, (quoniam, ut video, tormenta, non
scholas, parant antistites), rationem facti mei vobis
ut probarem; capita rerum, quae mihi tantum fidentiae pepererunt, quasi digito fontes ostenderem.
Vos etiam hortarer, quorum interest praeter caeteros, incumbatis in hanc curam, quam a vobis Christus, Ecclesia, respublica et vestra salus exigunt.
Ego si fretus ingenio, litteris, arte, lectione, memoria, peritissimum quemque adversarium provocavi

fui vanissimus et superbissimus, qui neque me, neque illos inspexerim; sin causam intuitus, existimavi satis me valentem esse, qui docerem hunc solem meridie lucere, debetis mihi fervorem istum concedere, quem honor Iesu Christi, Regis mei, et invicta veritas imperarunt. Scitis M. Tullium in Quintiana, quum Roscius victoriam adpromitteret, si efficeret argumentis, septingenta millia passuum non esse decursa biduo, non modo nihil veritum articulos et nervos Hortensii, sed ne grandiores quidem Hortensio, Phillipos, et Cottas, et Antonios, et Crassos, quibus maximam dicendi gloriam tribuebat, metuere potuisse. Est enim quaedam veritas tam illustris et perspicua, ut eam nullae verborum rerumque praestigiae possint obruere. Porro liquidius est quod nos agimus, quam illa fuit hypothesis Rosciana. Nam si hoc praestitero: coelos esse, divos esse, fidem esse, Christum esse, causam obtinui. Hic ego non sim animosus? Equidem occidi possum, superari non possum, iis enim Doctoribus insisto, quos ille Spiritus erudiit, qui nec fallitur, nec vincitur.

Quaeso a vobis ut salvi esse velitis. A quibus hoc impetraro, reliqua minime dubitanter expecto. Date modo vos huic sollicitudini, Christum obtestamini, industriam adiungite; profecto sentietis id, quod res est, et adversarios desperare, et nos, tam solide fundatos, quieto magnoque animo hanc arenam expetere oportere. Brevior hic sum, quod reliquo sermone vos alloquor. Valete.

RATIONES
OBLATI CERTAMINIS

Ego dabo vobis os et sapientiam, cui non poterunt resistere et contradicere omnes adversarii vestri. Luc. xxi. 15.

Rationum capita.
1. Sacrae Litterae.
2. Sacrarum Litterarum sententia.
3. Natura Ecclesiae.
4. Concilia.
5. Patres.
6. Firmamenta Patrum.
7. Historia.
8. Paradoxa.
9. Sophismata.
10. Omne genus testium.

PRIMA RATIO
SACRAE LITTERAE.

Quum multa sunt, quae adversariorum diffidentiam in causa loquuntur, tum nihil aeque atque sanctorum maiestas Bibliorum foedissime violata. Etenim qui, posteaquam reliquorum testium voces et suffragia contempserunt, eo sunt redacti nihilo secius, ut stare nequeant, nisi divinis ipsis codicibus vim et manus intulerint; ii se profecto declarant extrema fortuna confligere, et rebus iam desperatis ac perditis, experiri durissima velle atque ultima.

Manicheis[1] quid causae fuit, ut " Evangelium Matthei et Acta refigerent Apostolica? " Desperatio. His enim voluminibus cruciabantur, et qui Christum negaverant prognatum de Virgine, et qui Spiritum christianis tum primo coelitus illapsum finxerant quum ipsorum Paracletus, Persa nequissimus, erupisset. Quid Ebioniis,[2] ut omnes Pauli repudiarent epistolas? Desperatio. His enim suam dignitatiem retinentibus, antiquata circumcisio est, quam isti revocaverant. Quid Luthero[3] ut Epistolam Iacobi "contentiosam, tumidam, aridum, stramineam," flagitiosus apostata nominaret, et " indignam spiritu censeret apostolico? " Desperatio. Hoc enim scripto confessus miser atque disruptus est, quum " in sola fide iustitiam, constitueret." Quid Lutheri catulis, ut Tobiam, Ecclesiasticum, Machabaeos, et horum odio complures alios eadem calumnia comprehensos, e sincero canone repente dispungerent? Desperatio. His enim oraculis disertissime coarguuntur, quoties de angelorum patrocinio, quoties de arbitrii libertate, quoties de fidelibus vita defunctis, quoties de Divorum hominum intercessione disputant.

Itane vero? Tantum perversitatis, tantum audaciae? Quum Ecclesiam, concilia, cathedras, Patres, martyres, imperia, populos, leges, academias, historias, omnia vetustatis et sanctitatis vestigia conculcassent, scripto Dei verbo tantum controver-

[1] Aug. l. 28 contra Faust. c. 2 et de utilit. cred. c. 3.
[2] Iren. l. 1, c. 26.
[3] Lut. in novo test. german.; Praef. in ep. Iac.; vide etiam l. de capt. Babyl. cap. de extr. unct. et cent, Magd. 2 p. 58.

sias velle dirimere proclamassent, illud ipsum verbum, quod solum restiterat, exsectis e toto corpore tam multis, tam bonis, tam speciosis, partibus, delumbasse? Septem enim ipsos de veteri Testamento[1] codices, ut minuta dissimulem, calviniani praeciderunt; lutherani vero etiam epistolam Iacobi, et huius invidia quinque alias;[2] de quibus aliquando fuerat et alicubi controversum. His quoque libellum Estheris et tria capita Danielis adnumerant novissimi Genuenses; quae quidem Anabaptistae, istorum condiscipuli, iam pridem damnaverant atque deriserant.

Quanto modestius Augustinus,[3] qui sacrosanctum catalogum pertexens, non sibi neque alphabetum hebraicum, ut Iudaei; neque privatum spiritum, ut Sectarii, pro regula posuit; sed illum Spiritum, quo totum corpus Ecclesiae Christus animat. Quae quidem Ecclesia custos huius depositi, non magistra, quod haeretici cavillantur, thesaurum hunc universum quem Tridentina[4] Synodus est amplexa, vetustissimis olim conciliis publicitus vindicavit. Idem Augustinus,[5] de una Scripturarum particula speciatim disserens, inducere in animum non potest, librum Sapientiae, qui iam tum Ecclesiae calculo, temporum serie, priscorum testimonio instinctione fidelium, ut firmus et canonicus robur obtinuerat, cuiusquam temeritate vel susurro ex-

[1] Ii sunt Baruch, Tobias, Iudith, Sapientia, Ecclesiast., duo Machab.
[2] Ep. ad Hebr., Ep. Iudae, Ep. 2 Petri, Epist. 2 et 3 Ioan.
[3] De doctr. christ. l. 2 c. 3.
[4] Conc. Trid. sess. 4; vid. Melch. Can. l. 2 de loc, theol.
[5] De praedest, sanct. c. 14.

trudi extra canonem oportere. Quid ille nunc diceret, si viveret in terris, et Lutheros Calvinosque concerneret opifices bibliorum, qui sua lima politula et elegantula vetus novumque Testamentum raserint; neque Sapientiam tantum, sed et alia permulta de canonicorum librorum ordine segregaverint: ut quidquid ex horum officina non prodierit, illud ad omnibus phrenetico decreto tamquam incultum et horridum conspuatur?

Ad hoc tam dirum et exsecrabile perfugium qui descenderunt, ii certe licet in ore suorum assecularum volitent, sacerdotia nundinentur declamitent in concione, ferrum in catholicos, equuleum crucemque consciscant; tamen victi, abiecti, squalidi, prostrati sunt: quandoquidem arrepta virgula censoria, veluti arbitri sedentes honorarii, divinas ipsas tabulas, si quae ad stomachum non fecissent, obliterant. Ecquis est vel mediocriter institutus, qui talium cuniculos hostium reformidet? Qui homines quamprimum in corona vestra, eruditorum hominum, ad eiusmodi veteratorias artes, tamquam ad familiarem daemonem currerent, non aurium convicio sed strepitu pedum exciperentur. Quaererem ab eis, verbi gratia, quo iure corpus biblicum detruncent atque diripiant? Respondent: non se veras Scripturas exscindere, sed excernere supposititias. Quo iudice? Spiritu sancto. Hoc enim responsum a Calvino[1] praescribitur, ut Ecclesiae iudicium, quo spiritus examinantur, subterfugiat. Cur igitur alios alii lancinatis, quum omnes eodem Spiritu gloriemini?

[1] Instit. I. lib. I, c. 7, num. 4 et 5.

Calvinianorum spiritus recipit sex epistolas, quae spiritui non placent lutherano; freti tamen uterque sancto Spiritu. Anabaptistae historiam Iobi fabulam[1] appellant, tragicis et comicis legibus intermixtam. Qui sciunt? Spiritu docente. Castalio[2] mysticum illud Salomonis Canticum, quod ut paradisum animae, ut manna reconditum, ut opiparas in Christo delicias catholici admirantur, nihilo pluris quam cantilenam de anicula, et cum pedissequis aulae colloquium amatorium venereus furcifer aestimavit. Vnde hausit? A spiritu. In Apocalypsi Ioannis, cuius omnes apices excelsum aliquid et magnificum sonare confirmat Hieronymus,[3] tamen Lutherus[4] et Brentius et Kemnitius quiddam, nescio quid, difficiles aristarchi desiderant; eo scilicet propendentes, ut exautoretur. Quem percontati? Spiritum. Quatuor Evangelia fervore praepostero Lutherus[5] inter se committit, et prioribus tribus Epistolas Pauli longe praeferens, " unicum " deinceps " Evangelium Ioannis, pulchrum, verum, praecipuum " decernit esse nominandum; quippe qui, quod in ipso fuit, libenter etiam Apostolos suarum rixarum socios adscripsisset. Quo doctore? Spiritu. Quin etiam iste fraterculus[6] non dubitavit Evangelium Lucae petulanti stylo perstringere, quod in eo crebrius bona nobis virtutum opera

[1] Xistus Sen. l. 8, haer. 10.
[2] Praef. in Cant. Vide Bezam in sua praef. ante comm. Calv. in Iosue.
[3] Epist. ad Paulinum.
[4] Lut. praef. in Apoc.—Kemn. in exam. Conc. Trid. sess. 4.
[5] Praef. in nov. Test.
[6] Lut. serm. de Pharis. et Publ.

commendentur. Quem interrogavit? Spiritum. Theodorus Beza ex Lucae vigesimo secundo capite: " Hic calix, novum testamentum, in meo sanguine, qui (calix) pro vobis fundetur, ποτήριον ἐνχυνόμενον," ausus est ut corruptum vitiatumque traducere, quod haec oratio nullam expositionem, nisi de vino calicis converso in verum Christi sanguinem, patiatur. Quis indicavit? Spiritus. Denique quum omnia credant suo quisque spiritui, nomen sancti Spiritus horribili blasphemia mentiuntur. Qui sic agunt, nonne se produnt? Nonne facile refutantur? Nonne in concessu talium virorum, quales estis Academici, tenentur ac minimo negotio constringuntur? Cum his ego timeam pro fide catholica disputare, qui pessima fide voces non humanas, sed aethereas tractavere?

Nihil hic dico, quae vertendo perverterint quamvis intolerabilia sint, quae accusem. Gregorio Martino, scientissimo linguarum, collegae meo, qui doctius et plenius hoc praestabit, nihil praeripio, nec aliis, quibus id laboris esse iam prae manibus intellexi. Facinorosius crimen est ac tetrius, quod nunc persequor. Inventos esse doctorculos, qui temulento quodam impetu in coeleste chirographum involarint; idipsum pluribus locis, ut maculatum, ut mancum, ut falsum, ut subreptitium condemnarint; eius partes aliquas correxerint, aliquas corroserint, aliquas evulserint. Hinc omne propugnaculum, quo muniebatur, in lutheranos spiritus, tamquam in valla phantasmatum pictosque parietes commutarint; ne prorsus obmutescerent, quum in Scripturas, erroribus suis infestas, impingerent, quas nihilo commodius expedire, quam sorbere favillas, aut saxa mandere, potuissent.

Haec ergo mihi prima ratio vehemens et iusta fuit quae ubi partes adversarias umbraticas et fractas ostendisset, animum sane addidit viro et christiano et in his studiis exercitato, pro sempiterni Regis diplomate adversus reliquias profligatorum hostium decertandi.

SECVNDA RATIO
SACRARVM LITTERARVM SENTENTIA

Alterum est, quod me quidem ad congressum incitarit, et horum apud me copiolas elevarit, adversarii perpetuum in Scripturis exponendis ingenium, plenum fraudis, inane prudentiae. Statim haec, philosophi, tangeretis. Itaque vos auditores expetii.

Sciscitemur ab adversariis, exempli gratia, quidnam sequuti novam sectam intriverint, qua Christus excluditur e coena mystica? Si nominant Evangelium, accurrimus. A nobis verba sunt:[1] " Hoc est corpus meum. Hic est calix meus." Qui sermo visus est ipsi Luthero[2] tam potens, ut quum etiam discuperet fieri Zuinglianus, quod ea re plurimum incommodare Pontifici potuisset, captus tamen et victus apertissimo contextu, cederet; neque minus invitus Christum vere praesentem in Sacramento sanctissimo fateretur, quam olim daemones, victi miraculis, Christum Dei Filium vociferati sunt.[3]

[1] Matth. xxvi. 26; Marc. xiv. 22; Luc. xxii. 19.
[2] In epist. ad Argent.
[3] Matth. viii. 29; Marc. i. 24.

Agedum, pagella scripta superiores sumus; de sententia scripti contenditur. Hanc pervestigemus ex verbis adiacentibus:[1] "Corpus meum, quod pro vobis tradetur. Sanguis meus, qui pro multis effundetur." Adhuc durissimae partes Calvini sunt, nostrae faciles et explicatae. Quid amplius? Conferte Scripturas, inquiunt. Conspirant Evangelia,[2] Paulus adstipulatur; voces, clausulae, tota connexio panem, vinum, insigne miraculum, coeleste pabulum, carnem, corpus, sanguinem, reverenter ingeminant. Nihil aenigmaticum, nihil offusum caligine loquendi.

Tamen perstant adversarii, neque finem faciunt altercandi. Quid agimus? Opinor, audiatur antiquitas; et quod nos alteris alteri suspecti non possumus, illud omnium saeculorum veneranda canities, Christo propior, ab hac lite remotior, decidat arbitrio. Non ferunt: prodi se aiunt. Dei verbum purum, purum, inclamant; hominum commentarios aversantur. Insidiose inepte. Dei verbum perurgemus, obscurant; Divos testamur interpretes, obsistunt. In summa, sic instituunt, nisi reorum iudicio steteris, nullum iudicium fore.

Atque ita se gerunt in omni, quam exercemus, controversia, de infusa gratia, de inhaerente iustitia, de Ecclesia conspicua, de necessitate Baptismatis, de Sacramentis et Sacrificio, de piorum meritis, de spe et timore, de peccatis imparibus, de auctoritate Petri, de clavibus, de votis, de conciliis evangelicis,

---

[1] Luc. xxii. 19; Matth. xxvi. 28; Marc. xiv. 24.
[2] Ioan. vi.; Matth. xvi.; Marc. xiv.; Luc. xxii.; 1 Cor. x. et xi.

de caeteris. Scripturas neque paucas et ponderosas catholici passim in libris, in colloquiis, in templis, in schola citavimus atque discussimus; eluserunt. Veterum scholia graecorum et latinorum admovimus; abnuerunt. Quid tum denique? Doctor Martinus Lutherus, aut vero Phillippus, aut certe Zuinglius, aut sine dubio Calvinus et Bezza, fideliter enarrarunt. Egone quemquam vestrum existimem tam esse mucosis naribus, qui hoc artificium, monitus, non persentiscat? Quare fateor me scholas Academicas cupide requirere, ut inspectantibus vobis, calamistratos istos milites, in solem et pulverem e suis umbraculis evocatos, non meis viribus, qui cum vestris centesima parte non sum conferendus, sed valentissima causa et certissima veritate debilitem.

TERTIA RATIO

NATVRA ECCLESIAE

Audito iam Ecclesiae nomine, hostis expalluit. Sed tamen excogitavit quiddam, quod a vobis animadverti volo, ut falsi ruinam et inopiam cognoscatis. Senserat in Scripturis tum propheticis, tum apostolicis, ubique honorificam Ecclesiae fieri mentionem: vocari civitatem sanctam (Apoc. xxi. 10), fructiferam vineam (Ps. lxxix.9), montem excelsum (Isai. ii. 2), directam viam (Ibid.xxxv. 8), columbam unicam (Cant. vi. 8), regnum coeli (Matth. xiii. 24), sponsam (Cant. iv. 8), et corpus Christi (Eph. v. 23 et 1 Cor. xii. 12), firmamentum veri (1 Tim. iii. 15), multitudinem illam, cui Spiritus promissas instillet omnia salutaria (Ioan. xiv. 26):

illam, in quam universam nullae sint umquam fauces diaboli morsum letiferum impacturae (Matth. xvi. 18); illam, cui quicumque repugnet, quantumvis ore Christum praedicet, non magis Christi, quam publicanus aut ethnicus (Matth. xviii. 17), potiatur.

Non est ausus contravenire sonitu, videri noluit Ecclesiae, quam toties Scripturae commemorant, refragari; nomen callide retinuit, rem ipsam funditus, definiendo, sustulit. His enim proprietatibus delineavit Ecclesiam, quae penitus ipsam occulant, et dimotam a sensibus tamquam ideam platonicam, secretis obtutibus hominum perpaucorum subiiciant;[1] eorum tantummodo, qui singulariter afflati, corpus hoc aerium intelligentia comprehenderent, et huiusce sodalitatis participes subtili quodam oculo lustrarent. Vbi candor? Vbi simplicitas. Quae Scripturae, quae sensa, qui Patres, hoc penicillo depingunt Ecclesiam? Sunt Christi ad Asiaticas ecclesias (Apoc. i. 2, 3), sunt Petri, Pauli, Ioannis, aliorum ad diversos epistolae; frequentes in Actis Apostolicis inchoantur et propagantur ecclesiae (Act. viii. 10, 11 et seq.). Quid istae? Num soli Deo et sanctis hominibus, an christianis etiam cuiuscumque generis, manifestae?

Sed profecto durum telum necessitas est. Ignoscite. Nam qui saeculis omnino quindecim, non oppidam, non villam, non domum reperiunt imbutam doctrina sua, donec infelix monachus (Lutherus) incesto connubio votam Deo virginem funes-

---

[1] Calv. Instit. l. iv., c. 1, n. 2 et 3.

tasset; aut Helvetius gladiator (Zuinglius) in patriam coniurasset; aut stigmaticus perfuga (Calvinus) Genevam occupasset; ii coguntur Ecclesiam, si quam volent, in latebris venditare, et eos parentes asserere, quos nec ipsi noverint, neque mortalium quisquam aspexerit. Nisi forte gaudent maioribus illis, quos haereticos fuisse liquet, ut Aerio, Ioviniano, Vigilantio, Helvidio, Iconomachis, Berengario, Valdensibus, Lolhardo, Wiclefo, Hussio; a quibus pestifera quaedam fragmenta dogmatum emendicarint.

Nolite mirari, si fumulos istos non pertimui, quos, modo ad meridianam lucem venero, minime fuerit laboriosum dispellere. Haec est enim nostra sermocianatio. Dic mihi: subscribis Ecclesiae, quae saeculis anteactis viguit?—Omnino.—Obeamus ergo terras et tempora. Cui?—Coetui fidelium.—Quorum?—Nomina nesciuntur. sed constat plurimos exstitisse.—Constat? Quibus constat?—Deo.—Quis dicit?—Nos, qui divinitus edocti sumus.—Fabulae qui credam?—Si arderes fide, tam scires hoc, quam te vivere.

Spectatum admissi, risum teneatis?

Iuberi christianos omnes adiungere se Ecclesiae, cavere ne spiritali gladio trucidentur, in domo Dei pacem colore, huic animas credere columini veritatis, istic querelas omnes deponere, hinc eiectos habere pro ethnicis; nescire tamen tot centinis, tot homines, ubinam illa sit, quive huc pertineant? Vnum illud crepare in tenebris, ubi ubi sit Ecclesia, tantummodo sanctos et in aethera destinatos ea contineri? Ex quo fit ut, si quis imperium sui Praesulis detrectare velit, scelere solvatur, dummodo sibi persuadeat presbyterum in crimen incidisse, et ab Ecclesia protinus excidisse.

Quum scirem adversarios talia comminisci, quod nullius aetatis Ecclesiae consuessent, et orbatos tota re, velle tamen inter angustias vocabulum possidere, solabar me vestro acumine, atque adeo mihi pollicebar, fore ut quamprimum huiusmodi technas ex ipsorum confessione cerneretis, statim homines ingenui et cordati stultas argutias in vestram intextas perniciem exscinderetis.

QVARTA RATIO
CONCILIA

Gravis, Ecclesia nascente, quaestio de legitimis caeremoniis, quae credentium animos disturbavit, coacto Apostolorum et seniorum concilio, soluta est. Credidere parentibus filii, pastoribus oves, in haec verba mandantibus:[1] " Visum est Spiritui sancto et nobis." Sequuta sunt ad extirpandam haeresim, quae varia quibusque saeculis pullulavit, oecumenica veterum Concilia quatuor, tantae firmitudinis, ut iis ante annos mille singularis honos tamquam divinis vocibus, haberetur.[2] Non abibo longius. Etiam domi nostrae, comitiis regni eadem Concilia pristinum ius inviolatamque dignitatem obtinent. Haec citabo, teque ipsam,[3] Anglia, dulcissima patria, contestabor. Si, quemadmodum

[1] Act. xv. 28.
[2] Greg. l. I, ep. 24.
[3] Ang. I Elizab.

prae te fers, quatuor ista Concilia reverebere, summum honorem primae sedis Episcopo, id est, Petro, deferes:[1] incruentum corporis et sanguinis Christi sacrificium in altari recognosces:[2] beatos Martyres, divosque omnes coelites, ut pro te Christo supplicent, obsecrabis:[3] mulierosos apostatas ab infando concubitu et incestu publico coercebis:[4] multa facies, quae demoliris; multa, quae facis, infecta voles.[5] Porro Synodos aliorum temporum, nominatim vero Tridentinam, eiusdem auctoritatis ac fidei cum primis illis fuisse, quando usus venerit, demonstraturum me spondeo atque recipio.

Auctus igitur Conciliorum omnium valido et exquisito praesidio, cur non ingrediar in hanc palaestram animo tranquillo et praesenti, observaturus adversarium, quo se proripiat? Nam et evidentissima producam, quae distorquere non poterit, et probatissima, quae respuere non audebit.

Fortasse verbosius loquendo diem extrahere conabitur; sed ab intentis hominibus, si vos rego bene novi, nec aures nec oculos compilabit. Quod si quis erit omnino tam demens, qui se unum opponat Senatoribus orbis terrae, et iis quidem omni exceptione maioribus, sanctioribus, doctioribus, vetustioribus; libenter aspiciam illud os, quod ubi vobis ostendero, reliqua cogitationibus vestris relinquam. Interim hoc monebo; qui pleno Concilio, rite atque ordine consummato, momentum et pondus abrogat,

---

[1] Nic. can. vi.; Chalc. act. iv.; Const. c. 5.
[2] Ephes. conc. in epist. ad Nestor; Nic. c. xiv.
[3] Chalc. act. xi.
[4] Nic. conc. apud Soc. l. i. c. 8.
[5] Vide Chalc. can. iv., vii., xvi., xxiv.

videri mihi nullo consilio, nullo cerebro; neque solum in theologicis tardum, sed etiam in politicis inconsultum. Si umquam Dei Spiritus illuxit Ecclesiae, certe illud est tempus immitendi Numinis, quum omnium ecclesiarum, quae sunt in terris patentissimae, religio, maturitas, scientia, sapientia, dignitas, unam in urbem confluxerint, adhibitisque modis omnibus divinis et humanis, quibus indagari veritas possit, promissum implorent Spiritum,[1] quo salutariter et prudenter sanciat.

Prosiliat nunc aliquis factionis haereticae magistellus, attollat supercilia, suspendat nasum, frontem perfricet, iudicesque suos scurriliter ipse iudicet. Quos ille ludos, quos iocos dabit? Repertus est Lutherus,[2] qui diceret, anteferre se Consiliis duorum suffragia bonorum et eruditorum hominum (putatote suum et Phillippi), si quando in Christi nomine consensissent. O circulos! Repertus est Kemnitius,[3] qui concilium Tridentinum ad suos vertiginis importunae calculos exegerit; quid lucratus? Infamiam. Dum iste nictaverit, sepelietur cum Ario; Tridentina Synodus quo magis inveterascet, eo magis in dies eoque perennius efflorescet. Bone Deus! quae gentium varietas, qui delectus episcoporum totius orbis, qui regum et rerumpublicarum splendor, quae medulla theologorum, quae sanctitas, quae lacrymae, quae ieiunia, qui flores academici, quae linguae, quanta subtilitas, quantus labor, quam infinita lectio, quantae virtutum et stu-

---
[1] Matth. xviii. 20; Ioan. xiv. 26.
[2] Lib. de capt. Bab.
[3] Exam. Conc. Trid.

diorum divitiae augustum illud sacrarium impleverunt? Audivi ego Pontifices exsultantes, et in his Antonium, archiepiscopum Pragensem, a quo sum creatus presbyter, amplissimos et prudentissimos viros, quod in ea schola haesissent aliquot annis, ut nullum Ferdinandi Caesaris, cui multum debuerant, regalius et uberius in se beneficium colerent, quam hoc fuit quod in Tridentino gymnasio legati ex Pannonia consedissent. Intellexit hoc Caesar, qui reversis ita gratulatus est: "Aluimus vos in schola optima."

Huc invitati fide publica, cur non properarunt adversarii, ut eos palam refellerent, in quos ranunculi coaxant e cavernulis?—Hussio et Hieronymo fregere fidem, inquiunt—Qui?—Constantiensis Concilii proceres—Falsum est: nullam dedere. Sed nec in Hussium tamen animadversum fuisset, nisi homo perfidiosus et pestilens, retractus ex fuga, quam ei Sigismundus Imperator periculo capitis interdixerat, violatis etiam conditionibus, quas scripto pepigerat cum Caesare, vim omnem illius diplomatis enervasset. Fefellit Hussium praecipitata malitia. Iussus enim, quum barbaras in sua Bohemia tragoedias excitasset, semetipsum sistere Constantiae, despexit praerogativam Concilii; securitatem petiit a Caesare, Caesar obsignavit, christianus orbis resignavit maior Caesare. Redire ad mentem haeresiarcha noluit: periit. Hieronymus vero Pragensis furtim venit Constantiam, protectus a nemine; deprehensus comparuit, peroravit, habitus est perbenigne, liber abiit quo voluit, sanatus est, haeresim eiuravit, relapsus est, exustus est.

Quid toties unum exemplum de sexcentis exagitant? Repetant annales suos. Martinus ipse Lutherus (a. 1518) odium Dei et hominum, Augustae positus coram Cardinale Caietano, nonne quod potuit, eructavit, et Maximiliani litteris communitus excessit? Idem accitus Wormatiam (a. 1521), quum et Caesarem et plerosque Imperii principes haberet infensos, nonne Caesaris verbo tutus fuit? Postremo lutheranorum et zuinglianorum capita, praesente Carolo quinto, haereticorum hoste, victore, domino, nonne datis induciis confessiones suas innovatas exhibuere comitiis Augustanis, et sospites abiere? Haud secus litterae Tridentinae locupletissimas adversario cautiones providerant:[1] uti noluit. Nimirum se iactat in angulis, in quibus ubi tria verba graeca sonuerit, sapere videatur; abhorret a luce, quae litteratorem in numero poneret, et ad honesta subsellia devocaret. Catholicis Anglis tale chirographum impunitatis impetrent, si diligunt salutem animarum. Nos Hussium non causabimur; verbo Principis innixi, convolabimus.

Sed ut, unde sum egressus, eo regrediar, Concilia generalia mea sunt, primum, ultimum, media; his pugnabo. Hastam exspectet adversarius amentatam, quam avellere numquam poterit. Prosternatur in eo satanas, Christus vivat.

[1] Vide Conc. Trid. sess. 11, 15 et 18.

QVINTA RATIO

PATRES

Antiochiae, qua primum in urbe Christianorum nobile cognomentum increbuit, Doctores,[1] id est, eminentes theologi; et Prophetae, id est, concionatores perquam celebres, floruerunt. Huiusce generis " scribas et sapientes, doctos in regno Dei, nova promentes et vetera,"[2] Christum callentes et Moysem, Dominus ipse futuros gregi prospexerat. Hos, ingentis beneficii loco donatos, explodere, quanti maleficii est? Explosit adversarius. Quid ita? Quia stantibus illis, concidisset. Id ego quum pro certissimo comperissem, pugnam simpliciter exoptavi, non illam iocularem, qua turbae velitantur in compitis, sed istam severam et acrem, qua congredimur in vestris Philosophorum spatiis:

—pede pes, densusque viro vir.

Ad Patres si quando licebit accedere, confectum est praelium; tam sunt nostri, quam Gregorius ipse decimus tertius, filiorum Ecclesiae Pater amantissimus. Nam ut omittam loca sparsa, quae ex monumentis veterum conquisita, nostram fidem apposite affirmateque propugnant; tenemus horum integra volumina, quae de industria religionem, quam tuemur, evangelicam distincte copioseque dilucidant. Duplex Hierarchia Martyris Dionysii[3] quas classes,

---

[1] Act. xiii. 1; 1 Cor. xii. 28; Ephes. iv. 11; 1 Cor. xiv., 1 et seq.
[2] Matth. xiii. 52.
[3] S. Dion. Areop. de quo vide. 6 Syn. act. 4, Adon., Tren. in martyr. Turon., Syng., Suid., Metap.

quae sacra, quos ritus edocet? Pupugit ea res Lutherum[1] tam valde, ut huius opera " simillima somniis, nec non perniciosissima " iudicaret. Imitatus parentem Caussaeus,[2] nescio quis terrae filius, ex Gallia, non est veritus hunc Dionysium, inclytae gentis Apostolum, vocitare " delirum senem." Centuriatores[3] vehementer offendit Ignatius et Calvinum,[4] ut in eius epistolis " deformes naevos, et putidas naenias " hominum quisquiliae notarint. Censoribus[5] illis "fanaticum quiddam " Irenaeus edixit; Clemens auctor Stromatum " zizania faecesque protulit;"[6] reliqui Patres huius aevi, sane apostolici viri, " blasphemias et monstra posteris reliquerunt." In Tertulliano rapiunt avide, quod a nobis edocti, nobiscum communiter detestentur; sed meminerint libellum de Praescriptionibus,[7] qui nostri temporis sectarios tam insigniter perculit, numquam fuisse reprehensum. Hippolytus, Portuensis[8] episcopus, quam belle, quam clare Antichristi nervum, lutherana tempora, praemonstravit? Eum propterea " scriptorem infantissimum et larvam " nominant. Cyprianum, delicias et decus Africae, Gallicanus ille criticus[9] et Magdeburgici[10] " stupidum, et destitutum Deo, et depravatorem poenitentiae " nuncuparunt. Quid admisit? Scrip-

[1] Comm. in 1, 13, 17 Deut. Item in capt. Babyl.
[2] Dial. 5 et 11.
[3] Cent. 2, c. 10.
[4] Inst. l. 1, c. 13, n. 29.
[5] Cent. 2, c. 5.
[6] Cent. 1, l. 2, c. 10 et seq.
[7] Tert. l. de praescr. contr. haer.
[8] Orat. de cos. secul.
[9] Causs. dial. 8 et 11.
[10] Cent. 3, c. 4.

sit enim de virginibus, de lapsis, de unitate Ecclesiae tractationes euismodi, eas etiam epistolas Cornelio, Romano Pontifici, ut nisi fides huic martyri detrahatur, Petrus Martyr Vermilius, omnesque cum eo foederati, peiores adulteris et sacrilegis habeantur. Ac ne singulis insistam diutius, Patres huius saeculi damnantur omnes, " quippe qui doctrinam de poenitentia mire depravarint."[1] Quo pacto? Nam austeritas canonum, quae viguit ea tempestate, maiorem in modum displicet huic sectae plausibili, quae tricliniis aptior, quam templis, voluptarias aures titillare et pulvillos omni cubito[2] solet assuere.

Quid aetas proxima, quid peccavit? Chrysostomus et ii Patres " iustitiam fidei foede " videlicet " obscurarunt."[3] Nazianzenus, quem honoris causa, Theologum veteres appellarunt, Caussaeo[4] iudice, " Fabulator, quid affirmaret, nesciit." Ambrosius " a cacodaemone fascinatus est." Hieronymus " aeque damnatus, atque diabolus: iniuriosus Apostolo,[5] blasphemus, sceleratus, impius." " Vnus " Gregorio Massovio[6] " pluris est Calvinus, quam centum Augustini." Parum est, centum; Lutherus[7] " nihili facit adversum se mille Augustinos, mille Cyprianos, mille Ecclesias." Longius rem deducere, supervacaneum puto. Nam in hos, qui bac-

---

[1] Ibid.
[2] Ezech. xiii. 18.
[3] Praef. in Cent. 5.
[4] Dial. 6, 7, 8.
[5] Beza in act. c. 23, v. 3.
[6] Test. Stanch. l. de Trinit.
[7] Contr. Henr. reg. Angl.

chantur, quis miretur in Optatum, Athanasium, Hilarium, Cyrillos, Epiphanium, Basilium, Vincentium, Fulgentium, Leonem, Gregoriumque Romanum fuisse procacissimos?

Quamquam si datur ulla rebus iniustis iusta defensio, non inficior habere Patres, ubicumque incideris, quod isti, dum sibi consentiunt, necessario stomachentur. Etinem qui odere stata ieiunia, quo animo oportet esse in Basilium, Nazianzenum, Chrysostomum, qui de quadragesima et indictis ieiuniorum feriis, tamquam de rebus iam usitatis, conciones egregias publicarunt? Qui suas animas auro, libidine, crapula et ambitiosis conspectibus vendiderunt, possuntne non esse inimicissimi Basilio, Chrysostomo, Hieronymo, Augustino, quorum excellentes libri de monachorum instituto, regula, virtutibus, teruntur?

Qui captivam hominis voluntatem invexere, qui christiana funebria sustulere, qui Divorum reliquias incendere, sintne placabiles Augustino, qui de libero arbitrio libros tres, de cura pro mortuis unum, de miraculis ad Basilicas et memorias Martyrum prolixum caput nobilissimi operis[1] et conciones aliquot exaravit? Qui fidem suis captiunculis metiuntur, nonne succenseant Augustino, cuius est insignis epistola,[2] qua se profitetur antiquitati, consensioni, successioni perpetuae et Ecclesiae, quae sola inter tot haereses Catholicae nomen usucapione vindicat assentire?

---

[1] Lib. 22 de Civit. Dei c. 8 et serm. de divers. 34 et seq.
[2] Contr. ep. Man. quam vocant funda c. 4.

Optatus, Milevitanus episcopus, Donatianam partem revincit[1] ex communione Catholica; nequitiam accusat ex decreto Melchiadis (lib. 1); haeresim refutat ex ordine Romanorum Pontificum (lib. 2); insaniam patefacit ex Eucharistia et chrismate contaminatis (lib. 3); sacrilegium horret ex diffractis altaribus " in quibus Christi membra portata sunt," pollutisque calicibus " qui Christi sanguinem tenuerunt," (lib. 6). De Optato quid sentiant, aveo scire, quem Augustinus[2] ut venerabilem et catholicum episcopum, Ambrosio parem et Cypriano; quem Fulgentius[3] ut sanctum et fidelem Pauli interpretem, Augustini similem et Ambrosii, meminerunt.

Athanasii Symbolum in templis concinunt. Num favent ei, qui Antonium Eremitam Aegyptium,[4] gravis auctor, accurato libello dilaudaverit, quique cum Alexandrina Synodo[5] iudicium Sedis Apostolicae, Divi Petri, suppliciter appellarit? Prudentius in hymnis quoties precatur Martyres, quos decantat? Quoties ad eorum cineres et ossa Regem Martyrum veneratur? Num hunc probabunt? Hieronymus pro Divorum reliquiis et honoribus scribit in Vigilantium, in Iovinianum pro virginitatis gradu. Huccine patientur? Ambrosius[6] tutores suos Gervasium et Protasium, celebritate notissima, in Arianam ignominiam honestavit; cui facto divi-

[1] Lib. 1 contr. Parmen.
[2] Aug. l. 1. contr. Parmen.; De unit. c 16; et De doctr. christ. c. 40.
[3] Lib. 2 ad Monim.
[4] Vide S. Hieron. de Script. Eccles.
[5] Vide Epist. Syn. Alexandr. ad Felic. 2.
[6] Epist. ad Ital. Item serm. 91.

nissimi Patres[1] encomium tribuere: quod factum Deus non uno prodigio decoravit. Num benevoli sunt Ambrosio futuri? Gregorius Magnus, noster Apostolus, planissime noster est, eoque nomine nostris adversariis odiosus; quem Calvini[2] rabies negat in schola sancti Spiritus educatum, propterea quod sacras imagines illitteratorum libros appellasset.

Dies me deficeret numerantem epistolas, conciones, homilias, orationes, opuscula, disceptationes Patrum, in quibus ex apparato graviter et ornate nostra catholicorum dogmata roborarunt. Quamdiu apud bibliopolas ista venierint, tamdiu frustra nostrorum codices prohibentur; frustra servantur aditus oraeque maritimae; frustra domus, arcae, scrinia, capsulae disquiruntur; frustra tot portis minaces tabulae suffiguntur. Nullus enim Hardingus, nec Sanderus, nec Stapletonus, nec Bristolius haec nova somnia vehementius, quam hi, quos recensui, Patres, insectantur. Talia cogitanti accrevit animus et desiderium pugnae, in qua, quoquo se moverit adversarius, nisi gloriam Deo cesserit, feret incommodum. Patres admiserit, captus est; excluserit, nullus est.

Adolescentibus nobis ita contigit. Ioannes Ivellus antesignanus calvinianorum Angliae, catholicos ad Divi Pauli Londinensium incredibili iactantia lacessivit, invocatis per hypocrisim et imploratis Patribus, quicumque intra salutis annum sexcentesimum claruisset. Accipiunt conditionem memora-

---

[1] Aug. l. 22 de Civ. Dei; Greg. Tur. l. de glor, Mart. c. 46 et Metaph.
[2] Instit. l. 1, c. 11, n. 5.

biles viri, qui tum exsulabant Lovanii, summis licet difficultatibus propter iniquitatem suorum temporum circumsepti. Ausim dicere, tanto popularibus nostris bono fuisse illam Ivellii astutiam, inscitiam, improbitatem, impudentiam, quas ii scriptores feliciter expanderunt, ut vix aliud quidquam, memoria mea, provenerit Anglorum Ecclesiae laboranti fructuosius. Edictum continuo valvis appenditur, ne qui codices illiusmodi legerentur, neve haberentur. Quum tantis clamoribus propemodum extorti prodiissent, didicere quicumque negotium attigissent, Patres fuisse catholicos, id est, nostros. Neque hoc sibi suisque vulnus inflictum Laurentius Humfredus[1] tacuit; qui quum alte Ivellum quoad caetera sustulisset, unam ei notam aspersit inconsiderantiae, quod Patrum calculos recepisset, quibuscum sibi nihil esse commercii, nec fore, sine ulla circuitione proloquitur.

Pertentavimus etiam familiariter aliquando Tobiam Matthaeum, qui nunc in concionibus dominatur, quem propter bonas artes et virtutum semina dileximus, ut responderet ingenue, possetne qui Patres assiduus lectitaret, istarum esse partium, quas ille suaserat. Retulit, non posse, si pariter eos legeret iisque crederet. Verissimum hoc verbum est, neque aliter eum nunc, aut Mattheum Huttonum, qui vir nominatus in paucis, versare Patres dicitur, aut reliquos adversarios, qui hoc faciunt, sentire arbitror.

Hactenus ergo securus in hanc aciem potui descendere, bellaturus cum iis, qui quasi auribus lupum teneant, aeternam causae maculam cogantur inu-

[1] Lib. de vita Ivelli.

rere, sive recusent Patres, sive deposcant. Nam in altero fugam adornant, in altero suffocantur.

SEXTA RATIO
FIRMAMENTVM PATRVM

Si quibus umquam cordi curaeque fuit id, quod maximopere nostris fuit et esse debet: "Scrutamini Scripturas,"[1] facile princeps et palmares in hoc genere sanctissimi Patres exstitere. Horum opera sumptuque tot gentibus et linguis transcripta Biblia et importata sunt; horum periculis et cruciatibus erepta de flammis hostilibus et vastitate; horum laboribus et vigiliis omnem in partem enucleata studiosissime; die noctuque sacras Litteras imbibere, de suggestibus omnibus sacras Litteras edidere, immensa volumina sacris Litteris ditavere, fidelissimis commentariis sacras Litteras explicuere cibos et inediam sacris Litteris condivere, occupati denique sacris in Litteris, ad senectutem decrepitam pervenere.

Quod si frequenter ipsi quoque ab auctoritate maiorum, ab Ecclesiae praxi, a successione Pontificum, a Conciliis oecumenicis, a traditionibus apostolicis, a cruore Martyrum, a scitis Praesulum, a visis eventisque mirabilibus argumentati sunt; tamen omnium maxime et libentissime sanctarum Litterarum testimonia densa conglobant, haec premunt, in his habitant, huic " armaturae fortium " duces robustissimi, sarta tecta civitatis Dei contra nefarios impetus quotidie munientes, optimo iure primas partes honoratissimasque porrigunt.

[1] Ioan. v. 39.

Quo magis demiror illam exceptionem adversarii superbam et fatuam, qui velut aquam in profluente quaeritans, sic in Scripturis confertissimis Scripturarum penuriam obiectat. Tantisper se Patribus assensurum dicit, dum sacris Litteris adhaerescunt. Num loquitur ex animo? Curabo igitur procedant armati atque stipati Christo, Prophetis, Apostolis atque omni apparatu biblico, celeberrimi auctores, antiquissimi Patres, sanctissimi viri, Dionysius, Cyprianus, Athanasius, Basilius, Nazianzenus, Ambrosius, Hieronymus, Chrysostomus, Augustinus, latinusque Gregorius. Regnet in Anglia fides illa, quam hi Patres, amicissimi Scripturarum, ex Scripturis exstruunt. Quas afferunt, afferemus; quas conferunt, conferemus; quod inferunt, inferemus. Placet? Excrea, dic sodes—Minime vero, inquis, nisi recte exponant—Quid est hoc ipsum, recte? Arbitratu tuo. Nihilne pudet labyrinthi?

Ergo quum sperem in Academiis florentissimis consociatum iri bene multos, qui, non pingui Minerva, sed acuto iudicio in has controversias inspecturi sunt, et horum responsa nugatoria libraturi, laetus hunc diem campi praestolabor, ut qui contra sylvestres tumulos mendiculorum inermium nobilitatem et robur Ecclesiae Christi cogitem educere.

SEPTIMA RATIO
HISTORIA

Pristinam Ecclesiae faciem historia prisca retegit. Huc provoco. Certe antiquiores historici, quos etiam usurpant adversarii, fere numerantur Eusebius, Damasus, Hieronymus, Ruffinus, Orosius,

Socrates, Sozomenus, Theodoretus, Cassiodorus, Gregorius Turonensis, Vsuardus, Regino, Marianus Sigebertus, Zonaras, Cedrenus, Nicephorus. Quid narrant? Nostrorum laudes, progressus, vicissitudinem, hostes. Imo vero, quod observes diligenter, illi qui dissident a nobis odio capitali, Philippus, Pantaleon, Funecius, Magdeburgici, quum se ad scribendam vel chronologiam Ecclesiae vel historiam appulissent, nisi nostrorum gesta colligerent, ac inimicorum Ecclesiae nostrae fraudes et scelera coacervarent, mille quingentos annos argumento vacui praetermitterent.

Cum his considera peculiares certarum historiographos regionum, qui unius acta cuiusque populi curiosius operosiusque scrutati sunt. Ii quasi Spartam adepti, quam locupletare modis omnibus et perpolire cuperent, qui ne convivia quidem lautiora, aut manicatas tunicas, aut pugionum capulos, aut inaurata calcaria, talesque minutias, si novitatem saperent, tacuere; profecto, si quid in religione mutatum, aut a primis degeneratum saeculis inaudissent, frequentes memorassent; si non frequentes, saltem aliqui: si non aliqui, unus aliquis absque dubio. Nullus omnino, neque benevolus nobis, neque malevolus, non modo quidquam tale prodidit, sed nec significavit.

Verbi gratia. Dant nobis adversarii, nec aliter possunt, fuisse Romanam Ecclesiam aliquando Sanctam, Catholicam, Apostolicam: tum quum haec a Divo Paulo promeruisset elogia:[1] " Vestra fides annuntiatur in universo mundo: sine inter-

---

[1] Rom. 1, 8, 9,; xv. 29; xvi. 16, 19.

missione memoriam vestri facio: Scio quia veniens ad vos, in abundantia benedictionis Christi veniam: Salutant vos omnes Ecclesiae Christi: Vestra enim obedientia in omnem locum divulgata est." Tum quum ibi Paulus in libera custodia[1] disseminaret Evangelium; tum quum in ea quondam " Babylone coëlectam Ecclesiam "[2] Petrus regeret; tum quum ille Clemens,[3] apprime laudatus ab Apostolo,[4] sederet ad ipsa gubernacula; tum quum profani Caesares,[5] ut Nero, Domitianus, Traianus, Antoninus, Romanos Pontifices laniarent; tum etiam, vel Calvino[6] teste, quum Damasus, Siricius, Anastasius, Innocentius, clavum tenerent Apostolicum. Hoc enim saeculo nihil adhuc, praesertim Romae, digressos ab Evangelica doctrina, liberaliter ille concedit.

Quando igitur hanc fidem tantopere celebratam Roma perdidit? Quando esse desiit, quod ante fuit? Quo tempore, quo Pontifice, qua via, qua vi, quibus incrementis urbem et orbem religio pervasit aliena? Quas voces, quas turbas, quae lamenta progenuit? Omnes orbe reliquo sopiti sunt, dum Roma, Roma, inquam, nova sacramenta, novum sacrificium, novum religionis dogma procuderet? Nullus exstitit historicus neque latinus, neque graecus, neque remotus, neque citimus, qui rem tantam vel obscure iaceret in commentarios?

[1] Act. xxviii. 30.
[2] 1 Pet. v. 13.
[3] Hieron. in cap. script. Eccles.; Euseb. 2 hist.c, 14.
[4] Phillip. iv. 3.
[5] Iren. l. 3, c. 3.
[6] Inst. l. 4, c. 2, n. 3 et in epist. ad Sadol.

Ergo perspicuum hoc quidem est, si, quae nos credimus, historia multa et varia, nuntia vetustatis, vita memoriae, loquitur ac repetit affluenter; quae vero isti obtrudunt, nulla naratio post homines natos in Ecclesia valuisse commeminit: et Historicos esse meos, et incursiones adversarias esse frigidissimas, quae nihil movere possint, nisi prius receptum sit, omnes omnium temporum christianos in spissam perfidiam atque in gehennae voraginem corruisse, donec Lutherus Boram constuprasset.

OCTAVA RATIO

PARADOXA

Ego vero, praestantissimi viri, quum de multis haeresibus quaedam apud me opiniosissimorum portenta reputo, quae mihi venient expugnanda; meipsum inertiae nequitiaeque condemnem, si cuiusquam in experiundo facultatem aut vires extimescerem. Sit ingeniosus, sit eloquens, sit exercitatus, sit omnium librorum helluo; tamen aridus et balbus appareat necesse est, quum haec tam " adunata " sustentabit. Disputabitur enim, si forte nobis annuent, de Deo, de homine, de peccato, de iustitia, de sacrimentis, de moribus. Videro an ausint asseverare, quae sentiunt, quaeque, rebus addicti necessariis, divulgant in scriptiunculis. Faxo norint ista suorum axiomata.

DE DEO.—" Deus est auctor et causa[1] peccati, volens, suggerens, efficiens, iubens, operans, et in hoc impiorum scelerata consilia gubernans. Pro-

[1] Calv. Inst. l. 1, c. 18; l. 2, c. 4; l 3, cc. 23 et 24; Petr. Mart. in 1, Sam. 2.

prium Dei opus fuit,[1] ut vocatio Pauli, sic adulterium Davidis, Iudaeque proditoris impietas." Monstrum hoc, cuius Philippum aliquando puduit, Lutherus[2] tamen, a quo Philippus hauserat, quasi oraculum coeleste miris extollit laudibus, et alumnum suum eo nomine tantum non exaequat[3] Apostolo Paulo. Percontabor etiam, quid animi Luthero fuerit, quem Angli[4] calviniani " virum divinitus datum ad orbem illuminandum " pronuntiant, quum hunc versum demeret supplicationibus Ecclesiae.[5] " Sancta Trinitas, unus Deus, miserere nobis."

DE CHRISTO.—Mox ad personam Christi progrediar. Quaeram ista sibi quid velint; Christus Dei Filius, Deus de Deo? Calvino:[6] " Deus ex sese," Bezae:[7] " Non est genitus de Patris essentia." Item: " Duae constituantur in Christo uniones hypostaticae,[8] altera animae cum carne, Divinitatis cum humanitate altera." " Locus apud Ioannem:" ' Ego et Pater unum sumus,' non ostendit Christum Deum ' homoousion '[9] Deo Patri." Sed et 'anima mea, inquit Lutherus,[10] odit hoc verbum ' homoousion.' " Pergite: " Christus ab infantia

---

[1] Melanct. in cap. Rom. 8.
[2] Sic docet Luth. in asser. 36 et in resol. asser. 36 et in libr. de servo arbitrio.
[3] Praef. in Phillip. in ep. ad Rom.
[4] In Apol. Eccl. Anglic.
[5] Vide enchir. prec. an. 1541.
[6] Calv. Inst. l. 1, c. 13, n. 23, 24.
[7] Beza in Hes.
[8] Beza cont. Schmidel. l. de unitat. hypost. duas in Christ. nat.
[9] Calv. in Ioan. x, 30.
[10] Luth. contr. Latom,

non fuit gratia consummatus,[1] sed animi dotibus velut caeteri homines adolevit: usu factus quotidie sapientior, ita ut puerulus ignorantia laborarit." Quod perinde est, ac si dicerent originis labe et vitio sordidatum. Sed cognoscite diriora: "Christus, quum orans in horto, sudoribus aquae manaret et sanguinis, sensu damnationis aeternae cohorruit:[2] vocem edidit sine ratione, sine spiritu, vocem doloris impetu repentinam, quam, ut non satis meditatam, celeriter castigavit." Estne aliquid amplius? Attendite: "Christus, quum actus in crucem exclamaret:" 'Deus meus, Deus meus, ut quid dereliquisti me?' accensus est flammis inferni,[3] desperationis vocem emisit, non aliter affectus, quam si pereundum ei foret internecione sempiterna."

His etiam, si quid possunt, addant: "Christus, inquiunt,[4] descendit ad inferos, id est, mortuus gehennam gustavit, nihilo minus quam animae damnatorum, nisi quod sibi restituendus erat.—Quandoquidem enim morte corporea nobis nihil profuisset:[5] anima quoque luctari cum morte debuit aeterna, atque hoc modo nostrum scelus suppliciumque dependere." Ac ne quis forte suspicetur, istud Calvino per incuriam obrepsisse, idem Calvinus:[6] "Omnes vos, si qui doctrinam istam solatii

[1] Bucer. in Luc. 2; Calv. in har. ev.; Luc. Los.; Melanct. in ev. Dom. 1 p. Epiph.
[2] Marlorat. in Matth. 26; Calv. in harm. eveng.
[3] Brent. in Luc. part. 2, hom. 65 et in Ioan. hom. 54; Calv. in harm. evang.
[4] Schmidel. Conc. de pass. et coena Dom.; Aepinus comm. in Ps. 16.
[5] Calv. Inst. l. 2, c. 16, n. 10, 11; Brent. in catech, an. 1551.
[6] Ibid. n. 12.

plenam exagitastis, perditos" appellat "nebulones."
Tempora, tempora, cuiusmodi monstrum aluistis?
Cruor ille delicatus et regius, qui de innocentis
Agni corpore lacerato fissoque scaturiit, cuius cruoris una guttula propter dignitatem Hostiae mille
mundos redimere potuisset, nihil humano generi
profecit, nisi " mediator Dei et hominum (1 Tim.
ii. 5), homo Christus Iesus mortem quoque secundam (Apoc. ii. 11)," mortem animae, mortem gratiae, peccati solius et exsecrabilis blasphemiae
sociam, pertulisset? Prae hac insania modestus
videbitur Bucerus, quamquam est impudens, qui[1]
infernum in symbolo sepulcrum accipit, per epexegesim valde praeposteram, ac potius tautologiam
ineptam atque stolidam.

Anglicani sectarii, pars Calvino, idolo suo, pars
Bucero, magno magistro, solent accedere; pars
etiam submurmurant in hunc articulum, ne quid
facessat ultra molestiae, quemadmodum sine tumultu penitus eximatur de Symbolo. Id vero etiam
fuisse tentatum in conventiculo quodam Londinensi, memini narrasse mihi, qui interfuit, Richardum Chenaeum, miserrimum senem, male mulctatum a latronibus foris, neque tamen ingressum in
paternam domum. Hactenus de Christo.

DE HOMINE.—De homine[2] quid? " Imago Dei
penitus in homine deleta est, nulla boni scintilla
superstite: tota natura quoad omnes animae partes
ita funditus eversa, ut ne renatus quidem et sanctus

[1] Buc. in Matt. cap. 26.
[2] Illyr. in var. l. de orig. pecc.; Sarcer. de cons. vet.
Eccles.; Aepinus de imb. et pecc. Sanct.; Kemn. contra
cens. col.; Calv. Inst. l. 4, c. 15, n. 10, 11,

quidquam sit aliud intrinsecus, nisi mera corruptio atque contagio." Quorsum ista? Vt qui sola fide gloriam rapturi sunt, in omnium turpitudinum coeno volutati, naturam accusent, virtutem desperent, praecepta deonerent.

DE PECCATO.— Huc Illyricus, Magdeburgensium primipilus, illud suum adiecit immane placitum[1] de originis peccato, quod esse vult: " Intimam substantiam animarum, quippe quas, post Adami lapsum, diabolus ipse procreet, et in sese transformet." Hoc quoque tritum est in hac faece: " Omnia peccata esse paria:"[2] sed ita (ne Stoici reviviscant), " si Deo iudice ponderentur." Ac si Deus, aequissimus iudex, oneri nostro cumulum potius, quam levamentum faceret, et id, quod non est in re, quum sit ipse iustissimus, exaggeraret. Hac trutina non levius in Deum severissime iudicantem deliquerit ille caupo, qui gallum gallinaceum, quando non est opus, occiderit, quam infamis ille sicarius, qui plenus Beza, Gallum heroa Guisium, admiribili virtute principem, displosa fistula interemit; quo facinore nihil vidit orbis noster aetate nostra funestius, nihil luctuosius.

DE GRATIA.— Sed fortasse, qui tam sunt in peccati conditione tetrici, magnifice philosophantur de divina gratia, quae huic malo succurrere ac mederi possit. Praeclaras vero isti partes assignant gratiae, " quam neque infusam cordibus nostris, neque ad resistendum sceleribus validam esse latrant, sed

[1] Illyr. in var. l. de pecc. orig.—Vide Hesbusium in ep. ad Illyr.
[2] Calv. in antidot. Conc. Trid.—Idem docuerat Wiclef. apud. Wald. l. 2, de Sacr. c. 154.

extra nos in solo Dei favore[1] collocant:" qui favor non emendet impios, nec purget, nec illuminet, nec ditet; sed veterem illam sentinam adhuc manantem atque foetentem, ne deformis et odiosa putetur, Deo connivente, dissimulet. Quo suo plasmate tantopere delectantur, ut ne " Christus quidem aliter apud illos[2] gratia plenus et veritate dicatur, quam quod ei Deus Pater mirandum in modum faverit."

DE IVISTITIA.—Quae res ergo iustitia est? Relatio.[3] Non enim ex theologics concinnata virtutibus, fide, spe, charitate, quae animam suo nitore convestiant; sed tantum " occultatio delicti, quam qui sola fide prehenderit, ille tam de salute certus est, ac si iampridem interminato coeli gaudio[4] frueretur." Age, somniet hoc; sed unde constare poterit de futura perseverantia, qua qui caruit, exivit infelicissimus, licet ad tempus pure pieque iustitiam coluisset? Imo vero, " haec tua fides, Calvinus ait,[5] nisi tuam tibi perseverantiam firme pronuntiet, ut hallucinari nequeas, tamquam inanis et languida sperneretur." Agnosco discipulum Lutheri. "Christianus, inquit ille[6] etiam volens, non potest salutem perdere, nisi nolit credere."

DE SACRAMENTIS.—Ad Sacramenta festino. Nullum, nullum, non duo, non unum, O Sancte

---

[1] Luth. in resp. contra Lovan.
[2] Bucer. in Ioan. 1; Wald. in nat. Christi; Brent. hom 16 in Ioan ; Cent. l. 1, c. 4.
[3] Hesb. de iustif. in resp. asv. 115 obiect. Illyric. in Apol. confes. Antuerp. c. 6 de iustif.
[4] Calv. Inst. l. 3, c. 2, n. 28 etc.
[5] Calv. Inst. l. 3, c. 2, n. 40.
[6] Lib. de capt. Babyl.

Christe, reliquerant. Ipsorum quippe panis venenum est; Baptismus etsi adhuc verus, tamen ipsorum iudicio " nihil est, non est unda salutis, non est canalis gratiae, non derivat in nos Christi merita; sed significatio dumtaxat salutis est. Itaque nihilo pluris Baptismum Christi, quoad naturam rei, quam Ioannis facere caeremoniam. Si habeas, recte; si careas, nihil damni: crede, salvus es, antequam abluare."[1] Quid ergo parvuli, qui nisi iuventur virtute Sacramenti, sua fide miselli nihil assequuntur? " Potius quam Sacramento Baptismatis quidquam tribuamus, inquiunt Magdeburgici,[2] demus inesse fidem ipsis infantulis, qua serventur, cuius fidei pulsus quosdam abditos intelligant " ipsi, qui vivant necne, nondum intelligunt. Durum. Si hoc adeo durum est, Lutheri pharmacum auditote: " Praestat, inquit,[3] omittere, quandoquidem nisi credat infans, nequidquam lavatur." Haec illi quidem ancipites animo, quidnam enuntient categorice. Ergo Balthassar Pacimontanus diribitor interveniat; qui parens Anabaptistarum, quum parvulis motum fidei non posset affingere, Lutheri cantiunculam adprobavit, et paedobaptismum eiiciens e templis, " neminen nisi adultum fonte sacro decrevit abluere." Ad reliqua Sacramenta quod attinet, quamvis illa bestia multiceps horrendas eiectet contumelias, tamen quia quoti-

---

[1] Calv. Inst. l. 4, c. 15, n. 2 et 10; Cent. l. 1, c. 10; Luth. l. de capt. Babyl.
[2] Cent. 2 et 5, c. 4.
[3] Luth. adv. Cochlae, Item epist. ad Melanct. t. 2; et in ep. ad Wald.

dianae iam sunt et callum auribus obduxerunt, hic praetereo.

DE MORIBVS.—Restant haereticorum de vita et moribus frusta nocentissima, quae Lutherus evomit in chartas, ut ex unius pectoris impuro gurgustio pestem lectoribus inhalaret. Audite patienter, et erubescite, et mihi date veniam recitanti: " Si nolit uxor[1], aut non possit, veniat ancilla. Siquidem res uxoria tam est cuique necessaria, quam esca, potus, somnus. Matrimonium est virginitate multo praestantius; eam Christus, eam Paulus dissuaserunt hominibus christianis." Sed haec fortasse propria Lutheri sunt? Non sunt. Etiam nuper a meo Charco,[2] sed misere timideque defenduntur. Vultis ne plura? Quidni? " Quanto sceleratior es, inquit,[3] tanto vicinior gratiae. Omnes actiones bonae peccata sunt; Deo iudice, mortifera; Deo propitio, leviuscula[4]—Nemo malum suapte voluntate cogitat[5]—Decalogus nihil ad christianos[6]—Opera nostra Deus nequaquam curat—Soli recte participant coena Dominica, qui tristes, afflictas, perturbatas, confusas, erraticas apportant conscientias.—Confitenda crimina sunt, sed cuilibet, qui si te vel ioco absolverit, modo credideris, absolutus es.—Legere preces horarias non est sacerdotum, sed laicorum —Christiani liberi sunt a statutis hominum." Satis

---

[1] Luth. serm. de matrim. et lib. de vit. coniug.; in asser. art. 16; lib. de vot. monast.
[2] Charc. in Cens. suum.
[3] Luth. serm. de Pet.; in asser. art. 32.
[4] Id. l. de serv. arbit.
[5] Id. serm. de Moyse.
[6] Id. l. de capt. Bab. c. de Euch.

superque lacunam istam commosse videor. Iam finio. Nec vero putetis iniquiorem esse me, qui lutheranos et zuinglianos promiscue coarguerim; nam isti memores a quo proseminati sint, inter se fratres et amici volunt esse,[1] adeoque gravem interpretantur iniuriam, quum in ulla re praeter unam, discriminantur.

Equidem non sum tanti, ut vel mediocrem locum mihi sumam in selectis theologis, qui hodie bellum haeresibus indixere; sed hoc scio, quantuluscumque sum, periclitari me non posse, dum Christi gratia fultus adversum talia commenta, tam invisa, tam insulsa, tam bruta, coelo terraque iuvantibus, praeliabor.

NONA RATIO

SOPHISMATA

Scitum est, inter caecos luscum regnare posse. Apud rudes valet saepe fucata disputatio, quam schola Philosophorum exsibilat. Multa peccat adversarius in hoc genere; sed quatuor fallaciis plerumque consuitur, quas in Academia malim, quam in trivio, retexere.

Primum vitium σκιαμαχία est, quae auras et umbras magno contau diverberat. Hoc pacto: contra coelibes iuratos et votos in castimoniam, quod nuptiae bonae sint, virginitas melior, offeruntur Scripturae loquentes honorifice de coniugio. Quem feriunt? Contra meritum hominis christiani, tinctum Christi sanguine, alioquin nullum, promun-

---

[1] Apol. Eccles. Angl.

tur testimonia, quibus iubemur, nec naturae, nec legi, sed sanguini Christi fidere. Quem refellunt? In eos, qui colunt Coelites, ut famulos Christi maxime gratiosos, citantur integrae pagellae, quae vetant colere multos Deos. Vbinam sunt? Huiusmodi argumentis, quae apud haereticos infinita reperio, nobis esse detrimento non poterunt, vobis esse fastidio poterunt.

Aliud vitium λογομαχία est, quae sensa deserens, loquaciter cum verbo litigat, "Invenias mihi Missam, inquiunt, aut Purgatorium in Scripturis." Quid ergo? Trinitas, Homoousion, Persona, nusquam sunt in Bibliis, quia voces istae non sunt? Affine est huic peccato litterarum aucupium; quum neglecta consuetudine et mente loquentium, quae vita vocabuli est, adversus elementa contenditur. Nempe sic aiunt: "Presbyter nihil est Graecis, nisi senior; Sacramentum, quodvis mysterium." Caeterum acute D. Thomas,[1] ut omnia: "In vocibus, inquit, videndum, non tam ex quo, quam ad quid sumantur."

Tertium, ὁμωνυμία est, longe lateque patens. Vt: "Quorsum ordo sacerdotum, quum Ioannes (Apoc. v. 10) omnes nos vocaverit sacerdotes?" Etiam hoc addidit: "Regnabimus super terram." Quorsum ergo reges? Item: "Propheta (Isai. LVIII. 6) celebrat ieiunium spiritale, hoc est, ab inveteratis criminibus abstinentiam. Valeat ergo ciborum delectus, et dierum praescriptio." Siccine? Igitur insanierunt Moyses, David, Elias, Baptistes, Apostoli, qui biduo, triduo, vel

[1] In 1, p. q. 13, a. 2 ad 2.

hebdomadis inediam terminarunt; quae quidem, ut a crimine, debebat esse perpetua. Hoc quale sit, iam vidistis: propero.

Quartum his adiicitur " Circulatio," in hunc modum: Da mihi notas, inquam, Ecclesiae. " Verbum Dei et purissima Sacramenta." Haeccine sunt apud vos? " Quis dubitet?"—Ego vero pernego. " Consule verbum Dei."—Iam consului, minusque vobis, quam antea, faveo. " Attamen planum est." —Proba mihi. " Quia nos ne latum quidem unguem discedimus a verbo Dei."—Vbi est acumen tuum? Semperne capies pro argumento illud ipsum, quod ponitur in quaestione? Quoties hoc iam inculco? Num tu evigilas? Num faces admovendae sunt? Dico a te perperam exponi verbum Dei: testes habeo quindecim aetates, sta sententiae, non meae, non tuae, sed harum omnium.—" Stabo sententiae verbi Dei: Spiritus ubi vult, spirat." Eccum, quos gyros, quas rotas fabricat. Hic nugator, tot verborum atque sophismatum architectus, nescio cui formidolosus esse queat, molestus erit fortasse. Molestiam vestra prudentia sublevabit, formidinem res eripuit.

DECIMA RATIO

OMNE GENVS TESTIVM

" Haec erit vobis directa via, ita ut stulti non errent per eam."[1] Quis enim, quamvis hebes in plebecula, dummodo salutis cupidus parumper attenderit, semitam Ecclesiae tam egregie complanatam, non videat, non teneat; vepres, et cautes,

[1] Isai. xxxv. 8.

et avia detestatus? Erunt haec etiam rudibus explorata, sicut Isaias vaticinatus est; vobis igitur, si voletis, exploratissima.

COELITES.—Theatrum universitatis rerum ponamus ob oculos; quidquid est uspiam peragremus; omnia nobis argumenta suppeditant. Eamus in coelum: " Rosas[1] et lilia contemplemur," purpuratos nempe martyrio, candidatos innocentia. Romanos, inquam, Pontifices[2] tres et triginta continenter occisos; Pastores terris omnibus, qui suum pro Christi nomine sanguinem oppignerarunt; greges fidelium, qui Pastorum vestigiis institere; Divos omnes coelites, qui turbae hominum puritate et sanctimonia praeluxere. Nostros hic vixisse, nostros hinc emigrasse reperias. Noster fuit, ut paucula delibemus, ille martyrii sitientissimus Ignatius[3] " qui in rebus Ecclesiae neminem, ne regem[4] quidem, aequavit Episcopo: qui traditiones[5] quasdam Apostolicas, quarum testis ipse fuerat, ne dilaberentur, scripto mandavit." Noster anachoreta Telesphorus,[6] " qui ieiunium quadragesimale, sancitum ab Apostolis, observari severius iussit." Noster Irenaeus,[7] " qui a successione Cathedraque Romana fidem Apostolicam declaravit." Noster etiam Victor Pontifex, " qui[8] Asiam edicto coercuit universam:" quod quum aliquibus, atque etiam

[1] Aug. serm. 37 de Sanct.
[2] Dam. in vit. Pont. Rom.
[3] Hier. cat. Script.
[4] Ign. epist. ad Smyrn.
[5] Euseb. l. 3, c. 30.
[6] Dam. in vita Telesph. to. 1 con. c. stat. d. 5.
[7] Lib. 3, c. 3.
[8] Euseb. 5 hist. 24.

huic Irenaeo, viro sacratissimo, videretur asperius, nemo tamen attenuavit, ut exoticam potestatem. Noster Polycarpus,[1] qui super quaestione Paschatis Romam adiit, cuius ambustas reliquias Smyrna collegit, anniversario die rituque legitimo suum Episcopum venerata. Nostri Cornelius et Cyprianus,[2] aureum par Martyrum, ambo magni praesules; sed maior ille, qui Romanus Africanum errorem resciderat; hic nobilitatus observantia, qua maiorem est prosequutus, amicissimum sui. Noster Sixtus,[3] "cui ad aram solemnibus sacris operanti ministrarunt e clero septemviri." Noster Laurentius, huius Archidiaconus,[4] quem adversarii de suis fastis eiiciunt, quem ante mille ducentos annos vir consularis Prudentius[5] sic ornavit:

> Quae sit potestas credita
>   Et muneris quantum datum,
>   Probant Quiritum gaudia,
>   Quibus rogatus annuis.
> Hos inter, o Christi decus,
>   Audi et poetam rusticum,
>   Cordis fatentem crimina,
>   Et facta prodentem sua.
>   Audi benignus supplicem
>   Christi reum, Prudentium.

Nostrae virgines illae[6] perbeatae, Caecilia, Agatha, Anastasia, Barbara, Agnes, Lucia, Dorothea, Catharina; quae decretam pudicitiam adversus et homi-

---

[1] Euseb. 4 hist. 13 et 14.
[2] Euseb. 7 hist. 2 interp. Ruff.
[3] Prud. in hym. de S. Laur.
[4] Vid. Aug. Ser. 1 de S. Laur.; Ambr. l. 1 offi, c. 41; Leo serm. in die S. Laur.
[5] Prud. in hym. de S. Laur.
[6] Metaph.; Ambr. et alii.

num et daemonum tyrannidem firmaverunt. Nostra Helena, quam dominicae Crucis inventio celebravit. Nostra Monica, quae moriens[1] orari et sacrificari pro se mortua ad altare Christi, religiosissime flagitavit. Nostra Paula,[2] quae ex urbano palatio et opimis praediis in speluncam Bethleemiticam tantis itineribus peregrina cucurrit, ut ad Christi vagientis cunabula delitesceret. Nostri Paulus, Hilarion, Antonius, seniculi solitarii. Noster Satyrus,[3] Ambrosii germanus frater, qui tremendam illam hostiam circum se gestans in orario, naufragus insiliit in Oceanum, et fide plenissimus enatavit. Nostri Nicolaus et Martinus, episcopi, exerciti vigiliis, paludati ciliciis, ieiunio pasti. Noster Benedictus, tot monachorum pater. Chiliadas istas decennio non exsequerer.

Sed nec illos repeto, quos in Ecclesiae Doctoribus ante posueram. Memor sum brevitatis meae. Petat ista, qui volet, non solum ex abundanti veterum historia, sed multo etiam magis ex gravissimis auctoribus, qui paene singuli Divos singulos memoriae[4] reliquerunt. Renuntiet mihi, de christianis illis antiquissimis et beatissimis quid autumet? Vtrius doctrinae fuerint, catholicae, an lutheranae? Testor Dei solium et illud tribunal, ad quod stabo rationem rationum harum et dicti et facti redditurus, aut nullum coelum esse, aut nostrorum esse; illud exsecramur, hoc ergo defigimus.

[1] Aug. l. 6 confess. c. 7 ad 13.
[2] Hier. in epit. Paul.
[3] Ambr. in orat. fun. de Satyro.
[4] Vide sex tomos Surii de vitis Sanct.

DAMNATI.—Nunc e contrario, si libet, inspiciamus in Tartara. Cremantur incendio sempiterno. Qui? Iudaei. Quam Ecclesiam adversati? Nostram.—Qui? Ethnici. Quam Ecclesiam crudelissime persequuti? Nostram.—Qui? Turcae. Quae templa demoliti? Nostra.—Qui? Haeretici. Cuius Ecclesiae perduelles? Nostrae.—Quae enim Ecclesia praeter nostram omnibus inferorum portis[1] se opposuit?

IVDAEI.—Quum, pulsis Hebraeis, Christiani[2] succrescerent Hierosolymis, Deum immortalem! qui concursus hominum ad loca sacra fuit,[3] quae urbis religio, quae sepulcri, quae praesepii, quae crucis, quae monumentorum omnium, quibus velut exuviis mariti, Ecclesia sponsa delectatur? Hinc manavit in nos Iudaeorum odium ferum et implacabile. Queruntur etiam nunc, maiores nostros maioribus suis exitio fuisse. A Simone Mago et lutheranis nullum ictum acceperunt.

ETHNICI.—In Ethnicis violentissimi fuere, qui toto Imperio, trecentis annis, per intervalla temporum, aerumnosissima Christianis supplicia machinati sunt. Quibus? Patribus et filiis nostrae fidei. Cognoscite vocem tyranni, qui Divum Laurentium torruit in craticula:[4]

> Hunc esse vestris Orgiis
>   Moremque et artem, proditum est;
>   Hanc disciplinam foederis,
>   Libent ut auro antistites.

[1] Matth. xv. 18.
[2] Euseb. 4 hist. 5.
[3] Hieron, in epit. Paul. et passim in epist.
[4] Prudent. in hym. de S. Laur.

Argenteis scyphis ferunt
　Fumare sacrum sanguinem,
　Auroque nocturnis sacris
　Adstare fixos cereos.
Tunc cura summa est fratribus,
　(Vt sermo testatur loquax),
　Offerre, fundis venditis,
　Sestertiorum millia.
Addicta avorum praedia
　Foedis sub auctionibus
　Successor exhaeres gemit,
　Sanctis egens parentibus.
Haec occulantur abditis
　Ecclesiarum in angulis;
　Et summa pietas creditur
　Nudare dulces liberos.
Deprome thesauros, malis
　Suadendo quos praestigiis
　Exaggeratos obtines,
　Nigrantes quos claudis specu.
Hoc poscit usus publicus;
　Hoc fiscus, hoc aerarium,
　Vt dedita stipendiis
　Ducem iuvet pecunia.
Sic dogma vestrum est, audio;
　" Suum quibusque reddito."
　En Caesar agnoscit suum
　Numisma, nummis inditum.
Quod Caesaris scis, Caesari
　Da: nempe iustum postulo,
　Ni fallor; haud ullam tuus
　Signat Deus pecuniam.
Nec quum veniret, aureos
　Secum Philippos detulit;
　Praecepta sed verbis dedit
　　Inanis a marsupio.
Implete dictorum fidem,
　Quae vos per orbem venditis,
　Nummos libenter reddite;
　Estote verbis divites.

Quis videtur? In quos furit? Cuius Ecclesiae sacra, lychnos, ritus, ornamenta convellit? Cui patellas aureas, et argenteos calices, et sumptuosa donaria, et opulentam gazam invidet? Profecto lutherizat. Quod enim aliud velum suo latrocinio nostri Nemrodes[1] obtenderunt, quum depecularentur ecclesias, et Christi patrimonium dissiparent? Contra vero magnus ille Constantinus Christomastigon terror, quam Ecclesiam tranquillavit? Illam, cui Pontifex Sylvester praefuit,[2] quem in Soracte latitantem accersiit, ut eius opera nostro baptismate tingeretur.—Quibus auspiciis victor? Signo crucis.[3]—Qua matre gloriosus? Helena.—Quibus se patribus adiunxit? Nicaenis.—Cuiusmodi? Vt Sylvestro, ut Marco, ut Iulio, ut Athanasio, ut Nicolao.—Cuius se precibus[4] commendavit? Antonii. —Quam sellam postulavit[5] in Synodo? Vltimam. —O quanto regalior hac sede, quam qui regis titulum, non debitum, ambierunt! Singula narrare longum est. Sed ex his duobus altero nobis infestissimo, altero nobis amicissimo, licebit singula coniicere, quae sunt horum simillima. Etenim, ut nostrorum illa fuit Epistasis turbulenta, sic nostrorum haec evasit divina Catastrophe.

TVRCAE.—Turcica videamus. Mahometes et Sergius monachus apostata in profundo barathro iacent ululantes, et suis et posterorum sceleribus

[1] Gen. x. 9.
[2] Dam. in Sylv.; Niceph. l. 7, c. 33; Zonaras, Cedremus.
[3] Euseb. l. 2 de vit. Const. c. 7, 8, 9; Sozom. l. 1, c. 8, 9.
[4] Athan. in vita S. Ant.
[5] Theod. l. 1, hist. cap. 7.

onusti. Haec portentosa et efferata bellua, Sarraceni, Turcae, nisi a nostris ordinibus militiae sacrae,[1] nisi a nostris principibus et populis accisa fuisset ac repressa, per Lutherum quidem, (cui gratias hoc nomine Solymanus Turcus litteris egisse dicitur), et per lutheranos regulos (quibus Turcorum progressio laetabilis existimatur); haec, inquam, Erinnys furiosa et exitiosa mortalibus, totam iam depopularetur et vastaret Europam; neque indiligentius altaria et signa crucis, quam ipse Calvinus everteret. Ergo nostri hostes illi sunt proprii, utpote nostrorum industria a christianorum iugulis repulsi.

HAERETICI.—Despectemus in haereticos, faeces, et folles, et alimenta gehennae. Primus occurrit Simon Magus. Quid ille? "Eripiebat homini liberam[2] voluntatem; solam fidem[3] percrepabat." Mox Novatianus: Quis? Antipapa Cornelio,[4] Pontifici Romano, "hostis sacramentorum poenitentiae et chrismatis."[5] Deinde Manes Persa: hic docebat "baptismum salutem[6] non conferre." Post Aerius Arianus "preces damnabat pro mortuis,[7] confundebat episcopis sacerdotes." Hinc Aerius "solam[8] et ipse fidem personabat," cognominatus atheos[9] non minus quam Lucianus. Sequitur Vi-

---

[1] Vid. Volate, Iovium Aemilium l. 8, Blond. l. 9 de 2.
[2] Clem. l. 1, recog.
[3] Iren. l. 1, c. 2.
[4] Cypr. ep. ad Iubatam et l. 4 ep. 2.
[5] Theod. de fab. haeret.
[6] Aug. haer. 46, 53, 54.
[7] Epiph. haer. 75.
[8] Aug. haer. 54.
[9] Socr. l. 2, c. 28.

gilantius,[1] qui "Divos orari non ferebat:" ac Iovinianus, qui "virginitatem et nuptias aequiparabat." Denique colluvies universa Macedonius, Pelagius, Nestorius, Entyches, Monothelitae, Iconomachi, caeteri, quibus Lutherum et Calvinum posteritas aggregabit. Quid isti? Omnes mali corvi, eodem ovo geniti, ab Ecclesiae nostrae Praesulibus desciverunt, ab illis evicti et exinaniti sunt.

Deseramus avernum, reddamur terris. Quocumque me oculis et cogitatione convertero, sive Patriarchas intueor et sedes Apostolicas, sive Antistites caeterarum gentium, sive laudatos principes, reges, caesares, sive christianorum cuiusque nationis initia, sive ullum iudicium vetustatis, aut lumen rationis, aut honestatis decus; nostrae fidei serviunt et suffragantur omnia.

SEDES APOSTOLICA.—Testis Romana successio, "In qua semper Ecclesia, (ut cum Augustino ep. 162 loquar), Apostolicae Cathedrae viguit principatus." Testes illae reliquae sedes apostolicae, in quas hoc nomen insignite convenit, quod ab ipsis Apostolis horumve auditoribus exaedificatae[2] fuerint.

DISIVNCTTISSIMAE TERRAE.—Testes ubivis gentium pastores, loco dissiti, religione nostra concordes, Ignatius et Chrysostomus, Antiochiae; Petrus, Alexander, Athanasius, Theophilus, Alexandriae; Macharius et Cyrillus, Hierosolymis; Proclus, Constantinopoli; Gregorius et Basilius, in

---

[1] Hier. in Iovin. et Vigilant.; Aug. haer. 82.
[2] Vid. Tert. de praescr.; Aug. l. 2 de doctr. christ. c. 8.

Cappadocia; Thaumaturgus, in Ponto; Smyrnae, Polycarpus; Iustinus, Athenis; Dionysius, Corinthi; Gregorius, Nissae; Methodius, Tyri; Ephremus, in Cyria; Cyprianus, Optatus, Augustinus, in Africa; Epiphanius, in Cypro; Andreas, Cretae; Ambrosius, Paulinus, Gaudentius, Prosper, Faustus, Vigilius in Italia; Irenaeus, Martinus, Hilarius, Eucherius, Gregorius, Salvianus, in Gallia; Vincentius, Orosius, Ildefonsus, Leander, Isidorus, in Hispania; in Britannia, Fugatius, Damianus, Iustus, Mellitus, Beda. Denique, ne ambitiosus videar in nominibus, quaecumque vel opera, vel fragmenta supersunt eorum, qui disiunctissimis terris Evangelium severunt, omnia nobis unam fidem exhibent, quam hodie catholici profitemur. Christe, quid causae tibi afferam, quo minus me de tuis extermines, si tot luminibus Ecclesiae tenebricosos homulos, paucos, indoctos, dissectos, improbos, antetulero?

PRINCIPES.—Testes item principes, reges, caesares, horumque respublicae, quorum et ipsorum pietas, et ditionum populi, et pacis bellique disciplina se penitus in hac nostra doctrina catholica fundaverunt. Hic ergo quos ab oriente Theodosios, quos ab occidente Carolos, quos Eduardos ex Anglia, Ludovicos e Gallia, Hermenegildos ex Hispania, Henricos a Saxonia, Wenceslaos e Bohemia, Leopoldos ex Austria, Stephanos ex Hungaria, Iosaphatos ex India, quos orbe toto dynastas atque toparchas possim arcessere; qui exemplo, qui armis qui legibus, qui sollicitudine, qui sumptu, nostram Ecclesiam nutrierunt? Sic enim praecinuit Isaias (xlix. 23): "Erunt reges nutricii tui, et reginae nutrices tuae." Audi, Elisabetha, Regina potentissima, tibi canit, te tuas partes edocet. Narro tibi: Calvinum et hos principes unum coelum capere non potest. His ergo te principibus adiunge, dignam maioribus, dignam ingenio, dignam litteris, dignam laudibus, dignam fortuna tua. Solum hoc de te molior ego et moliar, quidquid me fiet, cui, tamquam hosti capitis tui, toties iam isti patibulum ominantur. Salve bona crux. Veniet, Elisabetha, dies ille, ille dies, qui tibi liquido commonstrabit, utri te dilexerint, Societas Iesu, an Lutheri progenies. Pergo.

NATIONES AD CHRISTAM TRADVCTAE.—Testes iam omne sorae plagaeque mundi, quibus evangelica tuba post Christum natum insonuit. Parumne hoc fuit, idolis ora claudere, Dei regnum gentibus importare? Christum Lutherus, catholici Christum loquimur. "Num divisus est Christus?"[1] Minime. Aut nos, aut ille, falsum Christum loquimur. Quid ergo? Dicam. Christus ille sit, et illorum sit, quo Dagon[2] invecto cervices fregerit. Noster Christus opera nostrorum uti voluit, quum Ioves, Mercurios, Dianas, Phaebadas, et illam noctem saeculorum atram, Erebumque tristem, e tot populorum cordibus relegaret. Non est otium longinqua perquirere; finitima tantum atque domestica speculemur. Hiberni ex Patritio, Scoti ex Palladio, Angli ex Augustino, Romae sacratis, Roma missis, Romam venerantibus, fidem aut nullam, aut certe nostram,

[1] 1 Cor. i. 13.
[2] 1 Reg. v. 4.

id est, catholicam insuxerunt. Res aperta. Curro.

CVMVLVS TESTIVM.—Testes academiae, testes legum tabulae, testes vernaculi mores hominum, testes selectio caesarum et inauguratio, testes regum ritus et inunctio, testes equitum ordines, ipsaeque chlamydes, testes fenestrae, testes nummi, testes urbanae portae domusque civicae, testes avorum fructus et vita, testes res omnes et reculae, nullam in orbe religionem, nisi nostram, imis umquam radicibus insedisse.

Quae mihi quum suppeterent, et certe sic efficerent meditantem, ut his omnibus nuntium remittere christianis, et consociari cum perditissimis quibusque, videretur insolentis insaniae; non diffiteor, animatus sum et incensus ad conflictum, in quo nisi Divi de coelo deturbentur, et superbus Lucifer coelum recuperet, cadere numquam potero. Quo mihi sit aequior Charcus, qui me tam immaniter concerpit, si hanc animulam peccatricem, quam tanti Christus emit, viae tutae, viae certae, viae regiae malui credere, quam Calvinis scopulis dumetisve suspendere.

CONCLVSIO

Habetis a me, florentes Academici, hoc munusculum, contextum operis in itinere subcisivis. Animus fuit et purgare me vobis de arrogantia, et satisfacere de fiducia, et interim dum ab adversariis una mecum in scholas invitemini, quaedam apponere degustanda. Si aequam, si tutum, si honestum ducitis, haberi Lutherum, aut Calvinum, canonem Scripturae, mentem sancti Spiritus, normam Ecclesiae, Conciliorum Patrumque paedagogum, omnium denique testium et saeculorum Deum, nihil est quod sperem, vobis lectoribus vel auditoribus. Sin estis ii, quos apud animum formavi meum, philosophi occulati, amatores veri, simplicitatis, modestiae; hostes temeritatis, nugarum, sophismatum; facile diem in aprico videbitis, qui dieculam angusta rima dispicitis. Dicam libere, quod meus in vos amor, et vestrum periculum et rei magnitudo postulat. Non hoc nescit diabolus, vos istam lucem, si quando coeperitis oculos attolere, conspecturos. Cuius enim stuporis fuerit, antiquitati christianae Hammeros et Charcos anteponere? Sed sunt quaedam illecebrae lutheranae, quibus suum ille regnum amplificat, quibus ille tendiculis hamatus multos iani vestri ordinis inescavit. Quaenam? Aurum, gloria, deliciae, veneres. Contemnite. Quid enim aliud ista sunt, nisi terrarum ilia, canorus aer, propina vermium, bella sterquilinia? Spernite. Christus dives est, qui vos alet; Rex est, qui ornabit; lautus est, qui satiabit; speciosus est, qui felicitatum omnium cumulos largietur. Huic vos adscribite militanti, ut cum eo triumphos, vere doctissimi vereque clarissimi, reportetis. Valete. Cosmopoli 1581.

TRANSLATOR'S PREFACE.

This is no dry controversial divinity, but a sort of illuminated copy of *theses*, the call of a knight's trumpet challenging his antagonist to come forth. The Ten Reasons represent the ten *theses*, which Edmund Campion would fain have maintained in the Divinity School at Oxford against all comers, sharing, as he did to the full, the passion which his age felt and seems entirely to have lost, for such intellectual tournaments, as the natural means to bring out the truth and compose religious differences. The reader, then, must not be surprised to find in this little work quite as much of rhetoric as of logic; if he is unfriendly, he may say considerably more. Nor, if he knows anything of the controversial methods of the sixteenth century, will he be surprised at the vehemence of the language. Compared with his opponents, Luther for example, Edmund Campion is mere milk and honey. His book made a great stir: it is what a successful book must be, instinct with the spirit of the age in which and for which it was written.

The Protestant answer to the Ten Reasons was not given in the Divinity School at Oxford. It was the rack in the Tower, and the gibbet at Tyburn; and that answer was returned ere the year was out.

J.R.

Pope's Hall, Oxford,
   May 1910.

PREFACE.

Edmund Campion, to the Learned Members of the Universities of Oxford and Cambridge, Greeting.

Last year, Gentlemen, when in accordance with my calling in life I returned under orders to this Island, I found on the shore of England not a little wilder waves than those I had recently left behind me in the British Seas. As thereupon I made my way into the interior of England, I had no more familiar sight than that of unusual executions, no greater certainty than the uncertainty of threatening dangers. I gathered my wits together as best I could, remembering the cause which I was serving and the times in which I lived. And lest I might perhaps be arrested before I had got a hearing from any one, I at once put my purpose in writing, stating who I was, what was my errand, what war I thought of declaring and upon whom. I kept the original document on my person, that it might be taken with me, if I were taken. I deposited a copy with a friend, and this copy, without my knowledge, was shown to many. Adversaries took very ill the publication of the paper. What they particularly disliked and blamed was my having offered to hold the field alone against all comers in this matter of religion, though to be sure I should not have been alone had I disputed under a public safe conduct. Hanmer and Chartres have replied to my demands. What is the tenour of their reply? All off the point. The only honest

answer for them to give is one they will never give:
" We embrace the conditions, the Queen pledges
her word, come at once." Meanwhile they fill the
air with their cries: " Your conspiracy! your sedi-
tious proceedings! your arrogance! traitor! aye
marry, traitor! " The whole thing is absurd.
These men are not fools: why are they wasting
their pains and damaging their own reputation?
Nevertheless, in reply to these two gentlemen (one
of whom has chosen my paper to run at for his
amusement, the other more maliciously has confused the whole issue) there has recently been presented a very clear memorial setting forth all that
need be said about our Society and their calumnies
and the part that we are taking. The only course
left open to me (since as I see, it is tortures, not
academic disputations, that the high-priests are
making ready) was to make good to you the account
of my conduct; to show you the chief heads and
point my finger to the sources from whence I derive
this confidence; to exhort you also, as it is your
concern above others, to give to this business that
attention which Christ, the Church, the Common
Weal, and your own salvation demand of you. If
it were confidence in my own talents, erudition, art,
reading, memory, that led me to challenge all the
skill that could be brought against me, then were
I the vainest and proudest of mortals, not having
considered either myself or my opponents. But if,
with my cause before my eyes, I thought myself
competent to show that the sun here shines at noon-
day, you ought to allow in me that heat which the

honour of Jesus Christ, my King, and the unconquered force of truth have put upon me. You know how in Marcus Tullius's speech for Publius Quintius, when Roscius promised that he should win the case if he could make out by arguments that a journey of 700 miles had not been accomplished in two days, Cicero not only had no fear of all the force of the pleading of the opposing counsel, Hortensius, but could not have been afraid even of greater orators than Hortensius, men of the stamp of Cotta and Antonius and Crassus, whose reputation for speaking he set higher than that of all other men: for truth does sometimes stand out in so clear a light that no artifice of word or deed can hide it. Now the case on our side is clearer even than that position of Roscius. I have only to evince this, that there is a Heaven, that there is a God, that there is a Faith, that there is a Christ, and I have gained my cause. Standing on such ground should I not pluck up heart? I may be killed, beaten I cannot be. I take my stand on those Doctors, whom that Spirit has instructed who is neither deceived nor overcome I beg of you, consent to be saved. Of those from whom I obtain this consent I expect without the least doubt that all the rest will follow. Only give yourselves up to take interest in this inquiry, entreat Christ, add efforts of your own, and certainly you will perceive how the case lies, how our adversaries are in despair, and ourselves so solidly founded that we cannot but desire this conflict with serene and high courage. I am brief here, because I address you in the rest of my discourse.   Farewell.

FIRST REASON
HOLY WRIT

Of the many signs that tell of the adversaries' mistrust of their own cause, none declares it so loudly as the shameful outrage they put upon the majesty of the Holy Bible. After they have dismissed with scorn the utterances and suffrages of the rest of the witnesses, they are nevertheless brought to such straits that they cannot hold their own otherwise than by laying violent hands on the divine volumes themselves, thereby showing beyond all question that they are brought to their last stand, and are having recourse to the hardest and most extreme of expedients to retrieve their desperate and ruined fortunes. What induced the Manichees to tear out the Gospel of Matthew and the Acts of the Apostles? Despair. For these volumes were a torment to men who denied Christ's birth of a Virgin, and who pretended that the Spirit then first descended upon Christians when their peculiar Paraclete, a good-for-nothing Persian, made his appearance. What induced the Ebionites to reject all St. Paul's Epistles? Despair. For while those Letters kept their credit, the custom of circumcision, which these men had reintroduced, was set aside as an anachronism. What induced that crime-laden apostate Luther to call the Epistle of James contentious, turgid, arid, a thing of straw, and unworthy of the Apostolic spirit? Despair. For by this writing the wretched man's argument of righteousness consisting in faith alone was stabbed through and rent assunder. What induced Luther's whelps to expunge off-hand from the genuine canon of Scripture, Tobias, Ecclesiasticus, Maccabees, and, for hatred of these, several other books involved in the same false charge? Despair. For by these Oracles they are most manifestly confuted whenever they argue about the patronage of Angels, about free will, about the faithful departed, about the intercession of Saints. Is it possible? So much perversity, so much audacity? After trampling underfoot Church, Councils, Episcopal Sees, Fathers, Martyrs, Potentates, Peoples, Laws, Universities, Histories, all vestiges of Antiquity and Sanctity, and declaring that they would settle their disputes by the written word of God alone, to think that they should have emasculated that same Word, which alone was left, by cutting out of the whole body so many excellent and goodly parts! Seven whole books, to ignore lesser diminutions, have the Calvinists cut out of the Old Testament. The Lutherans take away the Epistle of James besides, and, in their dislike of that, five other Epistles, about which there had been controversy of old in certain places and times. To the number of these the latest authorities at Geneva add the book of Esther and about three chapters of Daniel, which their fellow-disciples, the Anabaptists, had some time before condemned and derided. How much greater was the modesty of Augustine (*De doct. Christ. lib.* 2, *c.* 8.), who, in making his catalogue of the Sacred Books, did not take for his rule the Hebrew Alphabet, like the Jews, nor private judgment, like the Sectaries, but that Spirit wherewith Christ animates the whole Church. The Church, the guardian of this treasure, not its mistress (as heretics falsely make out), vindicated publicly in former times by very ancient Councils this entire treasure, which the Council of Trent has taken up and embraced. Augustine also in a special discussion on one small portion of Scripture cannot bring himself to think that any man's rash murmuring should be permitted to thrust out of the Canon the book of Wisdom, which even in his time had obtained a sure place as a well-authenticated and Canonical book in the reckoning of the Church, the judgment of ages, the testimony of ancients, and the sense of the faithful. What would he say now if he were alive on earth, and saw men like Luther and Calvin manufacturing Bibles, filing down Old and New Testament with a neat pretty little file of their own, setting aside, not the book of wisdom alone, but with it very many others from the list of Canonical Books? Thus whatever does not come out from their shop, by a mad decree, is liable to be spat upon by all as a rude and barbarous composition. They who have stooped to this dire and execrable way of saving themselves surely are beaten, overthrown, and flung rolling in the dust, for all their fine praises that are in the mouths of their admirers, for all their traffic in priesthoods, for all their bawling in pulpits, for all their sentencing of

Catholics to chains, rack and gallows. Seated in their armchairs as censors, as though any one had elected them to that office, they seize their pens and mark passages as spurious even in God's own Holy Writ, putting their pens through whatever they cannot stomach. Can any fairly educated man be afraid of battalions of such enemies? If in the midst of your learned body they had recourse to such trickster's arts, calling like wizards upon their familiar spirit, you would shout at them, —you would stamp your feet at them. For instance I would ask them what right they have to rend and mutilate the body of the Bible. They would answer that they do not cut out true Scriptures, but prune away supposititious accretions. By authority of what judge? By the Holy Ghost. This is the answer prescribed by Calvin (*Instit. lib.* I, *c.* 7), for escaping this judgment of the Church whereby spirits of prophesy are examined. Why then do some of you tear out one piece of Scripture, and others another, whereas you all boast of being led by the same Spirit? The Spirit of the Calvinists receives six Epistles which do not please the Lutheran Spirit, both all the while in full confidence reposing on the Holy Ghost. The Anabaptists call the book of Job a fable, intermixed with tragedy and comedy. How do they know? The Spirit has taught them. Whereas the Song of Solomon is admired by Catholics as a paradise of the soul, a hidden manna, and rich delight in Christ, Castalio, a lewd rogue, has reckoned it nothing better than a love-song about a mistress, and an amorous conversation with Court flunkeys. Whence drew he that intimation? From the Spirit. In the Apocalypse of John, every jot and tittle of which Jerane declares to bear some lofty and magnificent meaning, Luther and Brent and Kemnitz, critics hard to please, find something wanting, and are inclined to throw over the whole book. Whom have they consulted? The Spirit. Luther with preposterous heat pits the Four Gospels one against another (*Praef. in Nov. Test.*), and far prefers Paul's Epistles to the first three, while he declares the Gospel of St. John above the rest to be beautiful, true, and worthy of mention in the first place,—thereby enrolling even the Apostles, so far as in him lay, as having a hand in his quarrels. Who taught him to do that? The Spirit. Nay this imp of a friar has not hesitated in petulant style to assail Luke's Gospel because therein good and virtuous works are frequently commended to us. Whom did he consult? The Spirit. Theodore Beza has dared to carp at, as a corruption and perversion of the original, that mystical word from the twenty-second chapter of Luke, *this is the chalice, the new testament in my blood, which* (chalice) *shall be shed for you* ποτήριον ἐκχυνόμενον, because this language admits of no explanation other than that of the wine in the chalice being converted into the true blood of Christ. Who pointed that out? The Spirit. In short, in believing all things every man in the faith of his own spirit, they horribly belie and blaspheme the name of the Holy Ghost. So acting, do they not give themselves away? are they not easily refuted? In an assembly of learned men, such as yours, Gentlemen of the University, are they not caught and throttled without trouble? Should I be afraid on behalf of the Catholic faith to dispute with these men, who have handled with the utmost ill faith not human but heavenly utterances? I say nothing here of their perverse versions of Scripture, though I could accuse them in this respect of intolerable doings. I will not take the bread out of the mouth of that great linguist, my fellow-Collegian, Gregory Martin, who will do this work with more learning and abundance of detail than I could; nor from others whom I understand already to have that task in hand. More wicked and more abominable is the crime that I am now prosecuting, that there have been found upstart Doctors who have made a drunken onslaught on the handwriting that is of heaven; who have given judgment against it as being in many places defiled, defective, false, surreptitious; who have corrected some passages, tampered with others; torn out others; who have converted every bulwark wherewith it was guarded into Lutheran " spirits," what I may call phantom ramparts and parted walls. All this they have done that they might not be utterly dumbfounded by falling upon Scripture texts contrary to their errors, texts which they would have found it as hard to get over as to swallow hot ashes or chew stones. This then has been my First Reason, a strong and a just one. By revealing the shadowy and broken powers of the adverse faction, it has certainly given new courage to a Christian man, not unversed in these studies, to fight for the Letters Patent of the Eternal King against the remnant of a routed foe.

SECOND REASON
THE SENSE OF HOLY WRIT

Another thing to incite me to the encounter, and to disparage in my eyes the poor forces of the enemy, is the habit of mind which they continually display in their exposition of the Scriptures, full of deceit, void of wisdom. As philosophers, you would seize these points at once. Therefore I have desired to have you for my audience. Suppose, for example, we ask our adversaries on what ground they have concocted that novel and sectarian opinion which banishes Christ from the Mystic Supper. If they name the Gospel, we meet them promptly. On our side are the words, *this is my body, this is my blood*. This language seemed to Luther himself so forcible, that for all his strong desire to turn Zwinglian, thinking by that means to make it most awkward for the Pope, nevertheless he was caught and fast bound by this most open context, and gave in to it (*Luther, epistol. ad Argent.*), and confessed Christ truly present in the Most Holy Sacrament no less unwillingly than the demons of old, overcome by His miracles, cried aloud that He was Christ, the Son of God. Well then, the written text gives us the advantage: the dispute now turns on the sense of what is written.

Let us examine this from the words in the context, *my body which is given for you, my blood which shall be shed for many.* Still the explanation on Calvin's side is most hard, on ours easy and quite plain.

What further? Compare the Scriptures, they say, one with another. By all means. The Gospels agree, Paul concurs. The words, the clauses, the whole sentence reverently repeat living bread, signal miracle, heavenly food, flesh, body, blood. There is nothing enigmatical, nothing befogged with a mist of words. Still our adversaries hold on and make no end of altercation. What are we to do? I presume, Antiquity should be heard; and what we, two parties suspect of one another, cannot settle, let it be settled by the decision of venerable ancient men of all past ages, as being nearer Christ and further removed from this contention. They cannot stand that, they protest that they are being betrayed, they appeal to the word of God pure and simple, they turn away from the comments of men. Treacherous and fatuous excuse. We urge the word of God, they darken the meaning of it. We appeal to the witness of the Saints as interpreters, they withstand them. In short their position is that there shall be no trial, unless you stand by the judgment of the accused party. And so they behave in every controversy which we start. On infused grace, on inherent justice, on the visible Church, on the necessity of Baptism, on Sacraments and Sacrifice, on the merits of the good, on hope and fear, on the difference of guilt in sins, on the authority of Peter, on the keys, on vows, on the evangelical counsels, on other such points, we Catholics have cited and discussed Scripture texts not a few, and of much weight, everywhere in books, in meetings, in churches, in the Divinity School: they have eluded them. We have brought to bear upon them the *scholia* of the ancients, Greek and Latin: they have refused them. What then is their refuge? Doctor Martin Luther, or else Philip (Melancthon), or anyhow Zwingle, or beyond doubt Calvin and Besa have faithfully laid down the facts. Can I suppose any of you to be so dull of sense as not to perceive this artifice when he is told of it? Wherefore I must confess how earnestly I long for the University Schools as a place where, with you looking on, I could call those carpet-knights out of their delicious retreats into the heat and dust of action, and break their power, not by any strength of my own,—for I am not comparable, not one per cent., with the rest of our people,—but by force of a strong case and most certain truth.

THIRD REASON

THE NATURE OF THE CHURCH

At hearing the name of the Church the enemy has turned pale. Still he has devised some explanation which I wish you to notice, that you may observe the ruinous and poverty-stricken estate of falsehood. He was well aware that in the Scriptures, as well of Prophets as of Apostles, everywhere there is made honourable mention of the Church: that it is called the holy city, the fruitful vine, the high mountain, the straight way, the only dove, the kingdom of heaven, the spouse and body of Christ, the ground of truth, the multitude to whom the Spirit has been promised and into whom He breathes all truths that make for salvation; her on whom, taken as a whole, the devil's jaws are never to inflict a deadly bite; her against whom whoever rebels, however much he preach Christ with his mouth, has no more hold on Christ than the publican or the heathen. Such a loud pronouncement he dared not gainsay; he would not seem rebellious against a Church of which the Scriptures make such frequent mention: so he cunningly kept the name, while by his definition he utterly abolished the thing, He has depicted the Church with such properties as altogether hide her away, and leave her open to the secret gaze of a very few men, as though she were removed from the senses, like a Platonic Idea. They only could discern her, who by a singular inspiration had got the faculty of grasping with their intelligence this aerial body, and with keen eye regarding the members of such a company.

What has become of candour and straightforwardness? What Scripture texts or Scripture meanings or authorities of Fathers thus portray the Church? There are letters of Christ to the Asiatic Churches (Apoc. i. 3), letters of Peter, Paul, John, and others to various Churches; frequent mention in the Acts of the Apostles of the origin and spread of Churches. What of these Churches? Were they visible to God alone and holy men, or to Christians of every rank and degree? But, doubtless, necessity is a hard weapon. Pardon these subterfuges. Throughout the whole course of fifteen centuries these men find neither town, village, nor household professing their doctrine, until an unhappy monk by an incestuous marriage had deflowered a virgin vowed to God, or a Swiss gladiator had conspired against his country, or a branded runaway had occupied Geneva. These people, if they want to have a Church at all, are compelled to crack up a Church all hidden away; and to claim parents whom they themselves have never known, and no mortal has ever set eyes on. Perhaps they glory in the ancestry of men whom every one knows to have been heretics, such as Aerius, Jovinianus, Vigilantius, Helvidius, Berengarius, the Waldenses, the Lollards, Wycliffe, Huss, of whom they have begged sundry poisonous fragments of dogmas. Wonder not that I have no fear of their empty talk: once I can meet them in the noon-day, I shall have no trouble in dispelling such vapourings. Our conversation with them would take this line. Tell me, do you subscribe to the Church which flourished in bygone ages? Certainly. Let us traverse, then, different countries and periods. What Church? The assembly of the faithful. What faithful? Their names are unknown, but it is certain that there have been many of them. Certain? to whom is it certain? To God Who says so! We, who have been taught of God—stuff and nonsense, how am I to believe it? If you had the fire of faith in you, you would know it as well as you know you are alive. Let in as spectators, could you withhold your laughter? To think that all Christians should be bidden to join the Church; to beware of being cut down by the spiritual sword; to keep peace in the house of God; to trust their soul to the Church as to the pillar of truth; to lay all their complaints before the Church; to hold for heathen all who are cast out of the Church; and that nevertheless so many men for so many centuries should not know where the Church is or who belong to it! This much only they prate in the darkness, that wherever the Church is, only Saints and persons destined for heaven are contained in it. Hence it follows that whoever wishes to withdraw himself from the authority of his ecclesiastical superior has only to persuade himself that the priest has fallen into sin and is quite cut off from the Church. Knowing as I did that the adversaries were inventing these fictions, contrary to the customary sense of the Churches in all ages, and that, having lost the whole substance, they still wished in their difficulties to retain the name, I took comfort in the thought of your sagacity, and so promised myself that, as soon as ever you had cognisance of such artifices by their own confession, you would at once like men of mark and intelligence rend asunder the web of foolish sophistry woven for your undoing.

FOURTH REASON

COUNCILS

In the infant Church a grave question about lawful ceremonies, which troubled the minds of believers, was solved by the gathering of a Council of Apostles and elders. The Children believed their parents, the sheep their shepherds, commanding in their words, *It hath seemed good to the Holy Ghost and to us* (Acts xv). There followed for the extirpation of various heresies in various several ages, four Œcumenical Councils of the ancients, the doctrine whereof was so well established that a thousand years ago (see St. Gregory the Great's Epistles, lib. i. cap. 24) singular honour was paid to it as to an utterance of God. I will travel no further abroad. Even in our home, in Parliament (ann. 1 Elisabeth), the same Councils keep their former right and their dignity inviolate. These I will cite, and I will call thee, England, my sweet country, to witness. If, as thou professest, thou wilt reverence these four Councils, thou shalt give chief honour to the Bishop of the first See, that is to Peter: thou shalt recognise on the altar the unbloody sacrifice of the Body and Blood of Christ: thou shalt beseech the blessed martyrs and all the saints to intercede with Christ on thy behalf: thou shalt restrain womanish apostates from unnatural vice and public incest: thou shalt do many things that thou art undoing, and wish undone much that thou art doing. Furthermore, I promise and undertake to show, when opportunity offers, that the Synods of other ages, and notably the Synod of Trent, have been of the same authority and credence as the first. Armed therefore with the strong and choice support of all the Councils, why should I not enter into this arena with calmness and presence of mind, watchful to keep an eye on my adversary and see on what point he will show himself? I will produce testimonies most evident that he cannot wrest aside. Possibly he will take to scolding, and endeavour to talk against time, but he will not elude the eyes and ears of men who will watch him hard, as you will do, if you are the men I take you for. But if there shall be any one found so stark mad as to set his single self up as a match for the senators of the world, men whose greatness, holiness, learning and antiquity is beyond all exception, I shall be glad to look upon that face of impudence; and when I have shown it to you, I will leave the rest to your own thoughts. Meanwhile I will say thus much: The man who refuses consideration and weight to a Plenary Council, brought to a conclusion in due and orderly fashion, seems to me witless, brainless, a dullard in theology, and a fool in politics. If ever the Spirit of God has shone upon the Church, then surely is the time for the sending of divine aid, when the most manifest religiousness, ripeness of judgment, science, wisdom, dignity of all the Churches on earth have flocked together in one city, and with employment of all means, divine and human, for the investigation of truth, implore the promised Spirit that they may make wholesome and prudent decrees. Let there now leap to the front some mannikin master of an heretical faction, let him arch his eyebrows, turn up his nose, rub his forehead, and scurrilously take upon himself to judge his judges, what sport, what ridicule will he excite! There was found a Luther to say that he preferred to Councils the opinions of two godly and learned men (say his own and Philip Melanchthon's) when they agreed in the name of Christ. Oh what quackery! There was found a Kemnitz to try the Council of Trent by the standard of his own rude and giddy humour. What gained he thereby? Infamy. While he, unless he takes care, shall be buried with Arius, the Synod of Trent, the older it grows, shall flourish the more, day by day, and year by year. Good God! what variety of nations, what a choice assembly of Bishops of the whole world, what a splendid representation of Kings and Commonwealths, what a quintessence of theologians, what sanctity, what tears, what fears, what flowers of Universities, what tongues, what subtlety, what labour, what infinite reading, what wealth of virtues and of studies filled that august sanctuary! I have myself heard Bishops, eminent and prudent men,—and among them Antony, Archbishop of Prague, by whom I was made Priest,—exulting that they had attended such a school for some years; so that, much as they owed to Kaiser Ferdinand, they considered that he had shown them no more royal and abundant bounty than this of sending them to sit in that Academy of Trent as Legates from Bohemia. The Kaiser understood this, and on their return he welcomed them with the words, "We have kept you at a good school." Invited as our adversaries have been under a safe conduct, why have they not hastened thither, publicly to refute those against whom they go on quacking like frogs from their holes? "They broke their promise to Huss and Jerome," is their reply. Who broke it? "The Fathers of the Council of Constance." It is false; they never gave any promise. But anyhow, not even Huss would have been punished had not the perfidious and pestilent fellow been brought back from that flight which the Emperor Sigusmund had forbidden him under pain of death; had he not violated the conditions which he had agreed to in writing with the Kaiser and thereby nullified all the value of that safe-conduct. Huss's hasty wickedness played him false. For, having instigated deeds of savage violence in his native Bohemia, and being bidden thereupon to present himself at Constance, he despised the prerogative of the Council, and sought his safe-conduct of the Kaiser. Cæsar signed it; the Christian world, greater than Cæsar, cancelled the signature. The heresiarch refused to return to a sound mind, and so perished. As for Jerome of Prague, he came to Constance protected by no one; he was detected and arraigned; he spoke in his own behalf, was treated very kindly, went free whither he would; he was healed, abjured his heresy, relapsed, and was burnt. Why do they so often drag out one case in a thousand ? Let them read their own annals. Martin Luther himself, that abomination of God and men, was put in court at Augsburg before Cardinal Cajetan: there did he not belch out all he could, and then depart in safety, fortified with a letter of Maximilian? Likewise, when he was summoned to Worms, and had against him the Kaiser and most of the Princes of the Empire, was he not safe under the protection of the Kaiser's word? Lastly, at the Diet of Augsburg, in presence of Charles V., an enemy of heretics, flushed with victory, master of the situation, did not the heads of the Lutherans and Zwinglians, under truce, present their Confessions, so frequently re-edited, and depart in peace? Not otherwise had the letter from Trent provided most ample safe-guards for the adversary ; he would not take advantage of them. The fact is, he airs his condition in corners, where he expects to figure as a sage by coming out with three words of Greek: he shrinks from the light, which should place him in the number of men of letters [*litteratorum*] and call him to sit in honourable place. Let them obtain for English Catholics such a written promise of impunity, if they love the salvation of souls. We will not raise the instance of Huss: relying on the Sovereign's word, we will fly to Court. But, to return to the point whence I digressed, the General Councils are mine, the first, the last, and those between. With them I will fight. Let the adversary look for a javelin hurled with force, which he will never be able to pluck out. Let Satan be overthrown in him, and Christ live.

FIFTH REASON
FATHERS

At Antioch, in which city the noble surname of Christians first became common, there flourished *Doctors*, that is, eminent theologians, and *Prophets*, that is, very celebrated preachers (Acts xiii. 1). Of this sort were the *scribes and wise men, learned in the kingdom of God, bringing forth new things and old* (Matth. xiii. 52; xxiii. 34), knowing Christ and Moses, whom the Lord promised to His future flock. What a wicked thing it is to scout these teachers, given as they are by way of a mighty boon! The adversary has scouted them. Why? Because their standing means his fall. Having found that out for certain beyond doubt, I have asked for a fight unqualified, not that sham-fight in which the crowds in the street engage, and skirmish with one another, but the earnest and keen struggle in which we join in the arena of yon philosophers,

Foot to foot, and man close gripping man.

If ever we shall be allowed to turn to the Fathers, the battle is lost and won: they are as thoroughly ours as is Gregory XIII. himself, the loving Father of the children of the Church. To say nothing of isolated passages, which are gathered from the records of the ancients, apt and clear statements in defence of our faith, we hold entire volumes of these Fathers, which professedly illustrate in clear and abundant light the Gospel religion which we defend. Take the twofold *Hierarchy* of the martyr Dionysius, what classes, what sacrifices, what rites does he teach? This fact struck Luther so forcibly that he pronounced the works of this Father to be " such stuff as dreams are made of, and that of the most pernicious kind." In imitation of his parent, an obscure Frenchman, Caussée, has not hesitated to call this Dionysius, the Apostle of an illustrious nation, " an old dotard." Ignatius has given grievous offence to the Centuriators of Magdeburg, as also to Calvin, so that these men, the offscouring of mankind, have noted in his works " unsightly blemishes and tasteless prosings." In their judgment, Irenaeus has brought out " a fanatical production ": Clement, the author of the *Stromata,* has produced " Tares and dregs ": the other Fathers of this age, Apostolic men to be sure, " have left blasphemies and monstrosities to posterity." In Tertullian they eagerly seize upon what they have learned from us, in common with us, to detest; but they should remember that his book *On Prescriptions*, which has so signally smitten the heretics of our times, was never found fault with. How finely, how clearly, has Hippolytus, Bishop of Porto pointed out beforehand the power of Antichrist, the times of Luther! They call him, therefore, " a most babyish writer, an owl." Cyprian, the delight and glory of Africa, that French critic Caussée, and the Centuriators of Magdeburg, have termed "stupid, God-forsaken corrupter of repentance." What harm has he done ? He has written *On Virgins, On the Lapsed, On the Unity of the Church*, such treatises as also such letters to Cornelius, the Roman Pontiff, that, unless credence be withdrawn from this Martyr, Peter Martyr Vermilius and all his associates must count for worse than adulterers and men guilty of sacrilege. And, not to dwell longer on individuals, the Fathers of this age are all condemned " for wonderful corruption of the doctrine of repentance." How so? Because the austerity of the Canons in vogue at that time is particularly obnoxious to this plausible sect which, better fitted for dining-rooms than for churches, is wont to tickle voluptuous ears and to sew *cushions on every arm* (Ezech. xiii. 18). Take the next age, what offence has that committed? Chrysostom and those Fathers, forsooth, have " foully obscured the justice of faith." Gregory Nazianzen whom the ancients called eminently " the Theologian," is in the judgment of Caussée " a chatterbox, who did not know what he was saying." Ambrose was " under the spell of an evil demon." Jerome is " as damnable as the devil, injurious to the Apostle, a blasphemer, a wicked wretch." To Gregory Massow—" Calvin alone is worth more than a hundred Augustines." A hundred is a small number: Luther " reckons nothing of having against him a thousand Augustines, a thousand Cyprians, a thousand Churches." I think I need not carry the matter further. For when men rage against the above-mentioned Fathers, who can wonder at the impertinence of their language against Optatus, Hilary, the two Cyrils, Epiphanius,

Basil, Vincent, Fulgentius, Leo, and the Roman Gregory. However, if we grant any just defence of an unjust cause, I do not deny that the Fathers, wherever you light upon them, afford the party of our opponents matter they needs must disagree with, so long as they are consistent with themselves. Men who have appointed fast-days, how must they be minded in regard of Basil, Gregory Nazianzen, Leo, Chrysostom, who have published telling sermons on Lent and prescribed days of fasting as things already in customary use? Men who have sold their souls for gold, lust, drunkenness and ambitious display, can they be other than most hostile to Basil, Chrysostom, Jerome, Augustine, whose excellent books are in the hands of all, treating of the institute, rule, and virtues of monks? Men who have carried the human will into captivity, who have abolished Christian funerals, who have burnt the relics of Saints, can they possibly be reconciled to Augustine, who has composed three books on Free Will, one on Care for the Dead, besides sundry sermons and a long chapter in a noble work on the Miracles wrought at the Basilicas and Monuments of the Martyrs? Men who measure faith by their own quips and quirks, must they not be angry with Augustine, of whom there is extant a remarkable Letter against a Manichean, in which he professes himself to assent to Antiquity, to Consent, to Perpetuity of Succession, and to the Church which, alone among so many heresies, claims by prescriptive right the name of Catholic?

Optatus, Bishop of Milevis, refutes the Donatist faction by appeal to Catholic communion: he accuses their wickedness by appeal to the decree of Melchiades: he convicts their heresy by reference to the order of succession of Roman Pontiffs: he lays open their frenzy in their defilement of the Eucharist and of schism: he abhors their sacrilege in their breaking of altars " on which the members of Christ are borne," and their pollution of chalices " which have held the blood of Christ." I greatly desire to know what they think of Optatus, whom Augustine mentions as a venerable Catholic Bishop, the equal of Ambrose and of Cyprian; and Fulgentius as a holy and faithful interpreter of Paul, like unto Augustine and Ambrose. They sing in their churches the Creed of Athanasius. Do they stand by him? That grave anchor who has written an elaborate book in praise of the Egyptian hermit Antony, and who with the Synod of Alexandria suppliantly appealed to the judgment of the Apostolic See, the See of St. Peter. How often does Prudentius in his Hymns pray to the martyrs whose praises he sings! how often at their ashes and bones does he venerate the King of Martyrs! Will they approve his proceeding? Jerome writes against Vigilantius in defence of the relics of the Saints and the honours paid to them; as also against Jovinian for the rank to be allowed to virginity. Will they endure him? Ambrose honoured his patron saints Gervase and Protase with a most glorious solemnity by way of putting the Arians to shame. This action of his was praised by most godly Fathers, and God honoured it with more than one miracle. Are they going to take a kindly view of Ambrose here? Gregory the Great, our Apostle, is most manifestly with us, and therefore is a hateful personage to our adversaries. Calvin, in his rage, says that he was not brought up in the school of the Holy Ghost, seeing that he had called holy images the books of the illiterate.

Time would fail me were I to try to count up the Epistles, Sermons, Homilies, Orations, Opuscula and dissertations of the Fathers, in which they have laboriously, earnestly and with much learning supported the doctrines of us Catholics. As long as these works are for sale at the booksellers' shops, it will be vain to prohibit the writings of our controversialists; vain to keep watch at the ports and on the sea-coast; vain to search houses, boxes, desks, and book-chests; vain to set up so many threatening notices at the gates. No Harding, nor Sanders, nor Allen, nor Stapleton, nor Bristow, attack these new-fangled fancies with more vigour than do the Fathers whom I have enumerated. As I think over these and the like facts, my courage has grown and my ardour for battle, in which whatever way the adversary stirs, unless he will yield glory to God, he will be in straits. Let him admit the Fathers, he is caught: let him shut them out, he is undone.

When we were young men, the following incident occurred. John Jewell, a foremost champion of the Calvinists of England, with incredible arrogance challenged the Catholics at St. Paul's, London, invoking hypocritically and calling upon the

Fathers, who had flourished within the first six hundred years of Christianity. His wager was taken up by the illustrious men who were then in exile at Louvain, hemmed in though they were with very great difficulties by reason of the iniquity of their times. I venture to assert that that device of Jewell's, stupid, unconscionable, shameless as it was, qualities which those writers happily brought out, did so much good to our countrymen that scarcely anything in my recollection has turned out to the better advantage of the suffering English Church. At once an edict is hung up on the doors, forbidding the reading or retaining of any of those books, whereas they had come out, or were wrung out, I may almost say, by the outcry that Jewell had raised. The result was that all the persons interested in the matter came to understand that the Fathers were Catholics, that is to say, ours. Nor has Lawrence Humphrey passed over in silence this wound inflicted on him and his party. After high praise of Jewell in other respects, he fixes on him this role of inconsiderateness, that he admitted the reasonings of the Fathers, with whom Humphrey declares, without any beating about the bush, that he has nothing in common nor ever will have.

We also sounded once in familiar discourse Toby Matthews, now a leading preacher, whom we loved for his good accomplishments and the seeds of virtue in him; we asked him to answer honestly whether one who read the Fathers assiduously could belong to that party which he supported. He answered that he could not, if, besides reading, he also believed them.¹ This saying is most true; nor do I think that either he at the present time, or Matthew Hutten, a man of name, who is said to read the Fathers with an assiduity that few equal, or other adversaries who do the like, are otherwise minded.

Thus far I have been able to descend with security into this field of conflict, to wage war with men, who, as though they held a wolf by the ears, are compelled to brand their cause with an everlasting stigma of shame, whether they refuse the Fathers or whether they call for them. In the one case they are preparing to run away, in the other they are caught by the throat.

SIXTH REASON
THE GROUNDS OF ARGUMENT ASSUMED BY THE FATHERS

If ever any men took to heart and made their special care,—as men of our religion have made it and should make it their special care,—to observe the rule, *Search the Scriptures* (John v. 39), the holy Fathers easily come out first and take the palm for the matter of this observance. By their labour and at their expense Bibles have been transcribed and carried among so many nations and tongues: by the perils they have run and the tortures they

---

[1] Cf. Newman, *Lectures on Anglican Difficulties*, Lect. xii.: " I say, then, the writings of the Fathers, so far from prejudicing at least one man (J.H.N.) against the modern Church, have been singly and solely the one intellectual cause of his having renounced the religion in which he was born and submitted himself to her."

have endured the Sacred Volumes have been snatched from the flames and devastation spread by enemies: by their labours and vigils they have been explained in every detail. Night and day they drank in Holy Writ, from all pulpits they gave forth Holy Writ, with Holy Writ they enriched immense volumes, with most faithful commentaries they unfolded the sense of Holy Writ, with Holy Writ they seasoned alike their abstinence and their meals, finally, occupied about Holy Writ they arrived at decrepit old age. And if they also frequently have argued from the Authority of Elders, from the Practice of the Church, from the Succession of Pontiffs, from Œcumenical Councils, from Apostolic Traditions, from the Blood of Martyrs, from the decrees of Bishops, from Miracles, yet most persistently of all and most willingly do they set forth in close array the testimonies of Holy Writ: these they press home, on these they dwell, to this *armour of the strong* (Cant. iii. 7), for the best of reasons, is the first and the most honourable part assigned by these valiant leaders in their work of forgiving and keeping in repair the City of God against the assaults of the wicked.

Wherefore I do all the more wonder at that haughty and famous objection of the adversary, who, like one looking for water in a running stream, takes exception to the lack of Scripture texts in writings crowded with Scripture texts. He says he will agree with the Fathers so long as they keep close to Holy Scripture. Does he mean what he says? I will see then that there come forth, armed and begirt with Christ, with Prophets and Apostles, and with all array of Biblical erudition, those celebrated authors, those ancient Fathers, those holy men, Dionyius, Cyprian, Athanasius, Basil, Nazianzen, Ambrose, Jerome, Chrysostom, Augustine, and the Latin Gregory. Let that faith reign in England, Oh that it may reign! which these Fathers, dear lovers of the Scriptures, build up out of the Scriptures. The texts that they bring, we will bring: the texts they confer, we will confer: what they infer, we will infer. Are you agreed? Out with it and say so, please. Not a bit of it, he says, unless they expound rightly. What is this " rightly "? At your discretion. Are you not ashamed of the vicious circle?

Hopeful as I am that in flourishing Universities there will be gathered together a good number, who will be no dull spectators, but acute judges of these controversies and who will weigh for what they are worth the frivolous answers of our adversaries, I will gladly await this meeting-day, as one minded to lead forth against wooded hillocks [cf. Cicero *in Catilinam* ii. 11], covered with unarmed tramps, the nobility and strength of the Church of Christ.

SEVENTH REASON

HISTORY

Ancient History unveils the primitive face of the Church. To this I appeal. Certainly, the more ancient historians, whom our adversaries also habitually consult, are enumerated pretty well as follows: Eusebius, Damasus, Jerome, Rufinus, Orosius, Socrates, Sozomen, Theodoret, Cassiodorus, Gregory of Tours, Usuard, Regino, Marianus, Sigebert, Zonaras, Cedrinus, Nicephorus. What have they to tell? The praises of our religion, its progress, vicissitudes, enemies. Nay, and this is a point I would have you observe diligently, they who in deadly hatred dissent from us,—Melancthon, Pantaleon, Funck, the Centuriators of Magdeburg,—on applying themselves to write either the chronology or the history of the Church, if they did not get together the exploits of our heroes, and heap up the accounts of the frauds and crimes of the enemies of our Church, would pass by fifteen hundred years with no story to tell.

Along with the above-mentioned consider the local historians, who have searched with laborious curiosity into the transactions of some one particular nation. These men, wishing by all means to enrich and adorn the Sparta which they had gotten for their own, and to that effect not passing over in silence even such things as banquets of unusual splendour, or sleeved tunics, or hilts of daggers, or gilt spurs, and other such minutiae having any smack of revelry about them, surely, if they had heard of any change in religion, or any falling off from the standard of early ages, would have related it, many of them; or, if not many, at least several; if not several, some one anyhow. Not one, well-disposed or ill-disposed towards us, has related anything of the sort, or even dropped the slightest hint of the same.

For example. Our adversaries grant us,—they cannot do otherwise,—that the Roman Church was at one time holy, Catholic, Apostolic, at the time when it deserved these eulogiums from St. Paul: *Your faith is spoken of in the whole world. Without ceasing I make a commemoration of you. I know that when I come to you, I shall come in the abundance of the blessing of Christ. All the Churches of Christ salute you. Your obedience is published in every place* (Rom. i. 8, 9; xv. 29; xvi. 17, 19): at the time when Paul, being kept there in free custody, was spreading the gospel (Acts xxviii. 31): at the time when Peter once in that city was ruling *the Church gathered at Babylon* (1 Peter v. 13): at the time when that Clement, so singularly praised by the Apostle (Phil. iv. 3) was governing the Church: at the time when the pagan Cæsars, Nero, Domitian, Trajan, Antoninus, were butchering the Roman Pontiffs: also at the time when, as even Calvin bears witness, Damasus, Siricius, Anastasius and Innocent guided the Apostolic bark. For at this epoch he generously allows that men, at Rome particularly, had so far not swerved from Gospel teaching. When then did Rome lose this faith so highly celebrated? when did she cease to be what she was before? at what time, under what Pontiff, by what way, by what compulsion, by what increments, did a foreign religion come to pervade city and world? What outcries, what disturbances, what lamentations did it provoke? Were all mankind all over the rest of the world lulled to sleep, while Rome, Rome I say, was forging new Sacraments, a new Sacrifice, new religious dogma? Has there been found no historian, neither Greek nor Latin, neither far nor near, to fling out in his chronicles even an obscure hint of so remarkable a proceeding?

Therefore this much is clear, that the articles of our belief are what History, manifold and various, History the messenger of antiquity, and life of memory, utters and repeats in abundance; while no narrative penned in human times records that the doctrines foisted in by our opponents ever had any footing in the Church. It is clear, I say, that the historians are mine, and that the adversary's raids upon history are utterly without point. No impression can they make unless the assertion be first received, that all Christians of all ages had lapsed into gross infidelity and gone down to the abyss of hell, until such time as Luther entered into an unblessed union with Catherine Bora.

EIGHTH REASON
PARADOXES

For myself, most excellent Sirs, when, choosing out of many heresies, I think over in my mind certain portentous errors of self-opinionated men, errors that it will be incumbent on me to refute, I should condemn myself of want of spirit and discernment if in this trial of strength I were to be afraid of any man's ability or powers. Let him be able, let him be eloquent, let him be a practised disputant, let him be a devourer of all books, still his thought must dry up and his utterance fail him when he shall have to maintain such impossible positions as these. For we shall dispute, if perchance they will allow us, on God, on Christ, on Man, on Sin, on Justice, on Sacraments, on Morals. I shall see whether they will dare to speak out what they think, and what under the constraint of their situation they publish in their miserable writings. I will take care that they know these maxims of their teachers:—" God is the author and cause of evil, willing it, suggesting it, effecting it, commanding it, working it out, and guiding the guilty counsels of the wicked to this end. As the call of Paul, so the adultery of David, and the wickedness of the traitor Judas, was God's own work" (Calvin, *Institut*. i. 18; ii. 4; iii. 23, 24). This monstrous doctrine, of which Philip Melanchthon was for once ashamed, Luther however, of whom Philip had learned it, extols as an oracle from heaven with wonderful praises, and on that score puts his foster-child all but on an equality, with the Apostle Paul (Luther, *De servo arbitrio*). I will also enquire what was in Luther's mind, whom the English Calvinists pronounce to be "a man given of God for the enlightenment of the world," when he wished to take this versicle out of the Church's prayers, " Holy Trinity, one God, have mercy on us."

I will proceed to the person of Christ. I will ask what these words, " Christ the Son of God, God of God," mean to Calvin, who says, " God of Himself" (*Instit.* i. 13); or to Beza, who says, "He is not begotten of the essence of the Father" (Beza in Josue, nn. 23, 24). Again. Let there be set up two hypostate unions in Christ, one of His soul with His flesh, the other of His Divinity with His Humanity (Beza, *Contra Schmidel*). The passage in John x. 30, *I and the Father are one*, does not show Christ to be God, consubstantial with God the Father (Calvin on John x.), the fact is, says Luther, "my soul hates this word, *homousion*." Go on. Christ was not perfect in grace from His infancy, but grew in gifts of the soul like other men, and by experience daily became wiser, so that as a little child He laboured under ignorance (Melanchthon on the gospel for first Sunday after Epiphany). Which is as much as to say that He was defiled with the stain and vice of original sin. But observe still more direful utterances. When Christ, praying in the Garden, was streaming with a sweat of water and blood, He shuddered under a sense of eternal damnation, He uttered an irrational cry, an unspiritual cry, a sudden cry prompted by the force of His distress, which He quickly checked as not sufficiently premeditated (Marlorati in Matth. xxvi.; Calvin *in Harm. Evangel.*). Is there anything further? Attend. When Christ Crucified exclaimed, *My God, my God, why hast Thou forsaken me*, He was on fire with the flames of hell, He uttered a cry of despair, He felt exactly as if nothing were before Him but to perish in everlasting death (Calvin *in Harm. Evangel.*). To this also let them add something, if they can.

Christ, they say, descended into hell, that is, when dead, He tasted hell not otherwise than do the damned souls, except that He was destined to be restored to Himself: for since by His mere bodily death He would have profited us nothing, He needed in soul also to struggle with everlasting death, and in this way to pay the debt of our crime and our punishment. And lest any one might haply suspect that this theory had stolen upon Calvin unawares, the same Calvin calls *all of you who have repelled this doctrine, full as it is of comfort, God-forsaken boobies* (Institut. ii. 16). Times, times, what a monster you have reared! That delicate and royal Blood, which ran in a flood from the lacerated and torn Body of the innocent Lamb, one little drop of which Blood, for the dignity of the Victim, might have redeemed a thousand worlds, availed the human race nothing, unless *the mediator of God and men, the man Christ Jesus* (1 Tim. ii. 5) had borne also *the second death* (Apoc. xx. 6), the death of the soul, the death to grace, that accompaniment only of sin and damnable blasphemy! In comparison with this insanity, Bucer, impudent fellow that he is, will appear modest, for he (on Matth. xxvi.), by an explanation very preposterous, or rather, an inept and stupid tautology, takes *hell* in the creed to mean the tomb. Of the Anglican sectaries, some are wont to adhere to their idol, Calvin, others to their great master, Bucer; some also murmur in an undertone against this article, wishing that it may be quietly removed altogether from the Creed, that it may give no more trouble. Nay, this was actually tried in a meeting at London, as I remember being told by one who was present, Richard Cheyne, a miserable old man, who was badly mauled by robbers outside, and, for all that, never entered his father's house.[1]

And thus far of Christ. What of Man? The image of God is utterly blotted out in man, not the slightest spark of good is left: his whole nature in all the parts of his soul is so thoroughly overturned that, even after he is born again and sanctified in baptism, there is nothing whatever within him but mere corruption and contagion. What does this lead up to? That they who mean to seize glory by faith alone may wallow in the filth of every turpitude, may accuse nature, despair of virtue, and discharge themselves of the commandments (Calvin, *Instit.* ii. 3). To this, Illyricus, the standard-bearer of the Magdeburg company, has added his own monstrous teaching about original sin, which he makes out to be the innermost substance of souls, whom, since Adam's fall, the devil himself engenders and transforms into himself. This also is a received maxim in this scum of evil doctrine, that all sins are equal, yet with this qualification (not to revive the Stoics), " if sins are weighed in the judgment of God." As if God, the most equitable Judge, were to add to our burden rather than lighten it; and, for all His justice, were to

---

[1] Richard Cheyne, Anglican bishop of Gloucester, to whom there is extant a letter from Campion, dated 1 November, 1571.

exaggerate and make it what it is not in itself. By this estimation, as heavy an offence would be committed against God, judging in all severity, by the innkeeper who has killed a barn-door cock, when he should not have done, as by that infamous assassin who, his head full of Beza, stealthily slew by the shot of a musket the French hero, the Duke of Guise, a Prince of admirable virtue, than which crime our world has seen in our age nothing more deadly, nothing more lamentable.

But perchance they who are so severe in the matter of sin philosophise magnificently on divine grace, as able to bring succour and remedy to this evil. Fine indeed is the function which they assign to grace, which their ranting preachers say is neither infused into our hearts, nor strong enough to resist sin, but lies wholly outside of us, and consists in the mere favour of God,—a favour which does not amend the wicked, nor cleanse, nor illuminate, nor enrich them, but, leaving still the old stinking ordure of their sin, dissembles it by God's connivance, that it be not counted unsightly and hateful. And with this their invention they are so delighted that, with them, even Christ is not otherwise called *full of grace and truth* than inasmuch as God the Father has borne wonderful favour to Him (Bucer on John i.: Brent hom. 12 on John).

What sort of thing then is righteousness? A relation. It is not made up of faith, hope and charity, vesting the soul in their splendour; it is only a hiding away of guilt, such that, whoever has seized upon this righteousness by faith alone, he is as sure of salvation as though he were already enjoying the unending joy of heaven. Well, let this dream pass: but how can one be sure of future perseverance, in the absence of which a man's exit would be most miserable, though for a time he had observed righteousness purely and piously? Nay, says Calvin (*Instit.* iii. 2), unless this your faith foretells you your perseverance assuredly, without possibility of hallucination, it must be cast aside as vain and feeble. I recognise the disciple of Luther. A Christian, said Luther (*De captivitate Babylonis*), cannot lose his salvation, even if he wanted, except by refusing to believe.

I hasten to pass on to the Sacraments. None, none, not two, not one, O holy Christ, have they left. Their bread is poison; and as for their baptism, though it is still true baptism, nevertheless in their judgment it is nothing, it is not a wave of salvation, it is not a channel of grace, it does not apply to us the merits of Christ, it is a mere token of salvation (Calvin, *Instit.* iv. 15). Thus they have made no more of the baptism of Christ, so far as the nature of the thing goes, than of the ceremony of John. If you have it, it is well; if you go without it, there is no loss suffered; believe, you are saved, before you are washed. What then of infants, who, unless they are aided by the virtue of the Sacrament, poor little things, gain nothing by any faith of their own? Rather than allow anything to the Sacrament of baptism, say the Magdeburg Centuriators (Cent. v. 4), let us grant that there is faith in the infants themselves, enough to save them; and that the said babies are aware of certain secret stirrings of this faith, albeit they are not yet aware whether they are alive or not. A hard nut to crack! If this is so very hard, listen to Luther's remedy. It is better, he says (*Advers. Cochl.*), to omit the baptism; since, unless the infant believes, to no purpose is it washed. This is what they say, doubtful in mind what absolutely to affirm. Therefore let Balthasar Pacimontanus step in to sort the votes. This father of the Anabaptists, unable to assign to infants any stirring of faith, approved Luther's suggestion; and, casting infant baptism out of the churches, resolved to wash at the sacred font none who was not grown up. For the rest of the Sacraments, though that many headed beast utters many insults, yet, seeing that they are now of daily occurrence, and our ears have grown callous to them, I here pass them over.

There remain the sayings of the heretics concerning life and morals, the noxious goblets which Luther has vomited on his pages, that out of the filthy hovel of his one breast he might breathe pestilence upon his readers. Listen patiently, and blush, and pardon me the recital. If the wife will not, or cannot, let the handmaid come (*Serm. de matrimon.*); seeing that commerce with a wife is as necessary to every man as food, drink, and sleep. Matrimony is much more excellent than virginity. Christ and Paul dissuaded men from virginity (*Liber de vot. evangel.*). But perhaps these doctrines are peculiar to Luther. They are not. They have been lately defended by my friend Chark, but miserably and timidly. Do you wish to hear any more? Certainly. The more wicked you are, he says, the nearer you are to grace (*Serm. de pisc. Petri*). All good actions are sins, in God's judgment, mortal sins; in God's mercy, venial. No one thinks evil of his own will. The Ten Commandments are nothing to Christians. God cares nought at all about our works. They alone rightly partake of the Lord's Supper, who bury consciences sad, afflicted, troubled, confused, erring. Sins are to be confessed, but to anyone you like; and if he absolves you even in joke, provided you believe, you are absolved. To read the Hours of the Divine Office is not the function of priests, but of laymen. Christians are free from the enactments of men (Luther, *De servo arbitrio, De captivitate Babylon*).

I think I have stirred up this puddle sufficiently. I now finish. Nor must you think me unfair for having turned my argument against Lutherans and Zwinglians indiscriminately. For, remembering their common parentage, they wish to be brothers and friends to one another; and they take it as a grave affront, whenever any distinction is drawn between them in any point but one. I am not of consequence enough to claim for myself so much as an undistinguished place among the select theologians who at this day have declared war on heresies: but this I know, that, puny as I am, I run no risk while, supported by the grace of Christ,

J

I shall do battle, with the aid of heaven and earth, against such fabrications as these, so odious, so tasteless, so stupid.

NINTH REASON
SOPHISMS

It is a shrewd saying that a one-eyed man may be king among the blind. With uneducated people a mock-proof has force which a school of philosophers dismisses with scorn. Many are the offences of the adversary under this head; but his case is made out by four fallacies chiefly, fallacies which I would rather unravel in the University than in a popular audience.

The first vice is σκιαμαχία, with mighty effort hammering at breezes and shadows. In this way: against such as have sworn to celibacy and vowed chastity, because, while marriage is good, virginity is better (1 Cor. vii.), Scripture texts are brought up speaking honourably of marriage. Whom do they hit? Against the merit of a Christian man, a merit dyed in the Blood of Christ, otherwise null, testimonies are alleged whereby we are bidden to put our trust neither in nature nor in the law, but in the Blood of Christ. Whom do they refute? Against those who worship Saints, as Christ's servants, especially acceptable to Him, whole pages are quoted, forbidding the worship of many gods? Where are these many gods? By such arguments, which I find in endless quantity in the writings of heretics, they cannot hurt us, they may bore you.

Another vice is λογομαχία, which leaves the sense, and wrangles loquaciously over the word. *Find me Mass or Purgatory in the Scriptures,* they say. What then? Trinity, Consubstantial, Person, are they nowhere in the Bible, because these words are not found? Allied to this fault is the catching at letters, when, to the neglect of usage and the mind of the speakers, war is waged on the letters of the alphabet. For instance, thus they say: *Presbyter to the Greeks means nothing else than elder; Sacrament, any mystery.* On this, as on all other points, St. Thomas shrewdly observes: " In words, we must look not whence they are derived, but to what meaning they are put."

The third vice is ὁμωνυμία, which has a very wide range. For example: *What is the meaning of an Order of Priests, when John has called us all priests?* (Apoc. v. 10). He has also added this: *we shall reign upon the earth.* What then is the use of Kings? Again: *the Prophet* (Isaias lviii.) *cries up a spiritual fast, that is, abstinence from inveterate crimes. Farewell then to any discernment of meats and prescription of days.* Indeed? Mad therefore were Moses, David, Elias, the Baptist, the Apostles, who terminated their fasts in two days, three days, or in so many weeks, which fasting, being from sin, ought to have been perpetual. You have already seen what manner of argument this is. I hasten on.

Added to the above is a fourth vice, Vicious Circle, in this way. Give me the notes, I say, of the Church. *The word of God and undefiled*

Sacraments. Are these with you? *Who can doubt it?* I do, I deny it utterly. *Consult the word of God.* I have consulted it, and I favour you less than before. *Ah, but it is plain.* Prove it to me. *Because we do not depart a nail's breadth from the word of God.* Where is your persecution? Will you always go on taking for an argument the very point that is called in question? How often have I insisted on this already? Do wake up: do you want torches applied to you? I say that your exposition of the word of God is perverse and mistaken: I have fifteen centuries to bear me witness: stand by an opinion, not mine, nor yours, but that of all these ages. *I will stand by the sentence of the word of God: the Spirit breatheth where it will* (John iii. 8). There he is at it again; what circumvolutions, what wheels he is making! This trifler, this arch-contriver of words and sophisms, I know not to whom he can be formidable: tiresome he possibly will be. His tiresomeness will find its corrective in your sagacity: all that was formidable about him facts have taken away.

TENTH REASON
ALL MANNER OF WITNESS

This shall be to you a straight way, so that fools shall not go astray in it (Isaias xxxv. 8).

Who is there, however small and lost in the crowd of illiterates, that, with a desire of salvation and some little attention, cannot see, cannot keep to the path of the Church, so admirably smoothed out, eschewing brambles and rocks and pathless wastes! For, as Isaias prophesies, this path shall be plain even to the uneducated; most plain therefore, if you choose, to you. Let us put before our eyes the theatre of the universe: let us wander everywhere: all things supply us with an argument. Let us go to heaven: let us contemplate roses and lilies, Saints empurpled with martyrdom or white with innocence: Roman Pontiffs, I say, three and thirty in a continuous line put to death: Pastors all the world over, who have pledged their blood for the name of Christ: Flocks of faithful, who have followed in the footsteps of their Pastors: all the Saints of heaven, who as shining lights in purity and holiness have gone before the crowd of mankind. You will find that these were ours when they lived on earth, ours when they passed away from this world. To cull a few instances, ours was that Ignatius, who in church matters put no one not even the Emperor, on a level with the Bishop; who committed to writing, that they might not be lost, certain Apostolic traditions of which he himself had been witness. Ours was that anchoret Telesphorus, who ordered the more strict observance of the fast of Lent established by the Apostles. Ours was Irenaeus, who declared the Apostolic faith by the Roman succession and chair (lib. iii. cap. 3). Ours was Pope Victor, who by an edict brought to order the whole of Asia; and though this proceeding seemed to some minds, and even to that holy man Irenaeus, somewhat harsh, yet no one made light of it as coming from a foreign power. Ours was Polycarp, who went to Rome on the question of Easter, whose burnt relics

Smyrna gathered, and honoured her Bishop with an anniversary feast and appointed ceremony. Ours were Cornelius and Cyprian, a golden pair of Martyrs, both great Bishops, but greater he, the Roman, who had rescinded the African error; while the latter was ennobled by the obedience which he paid to the elder, his very dear friend. Ours was Sixtus, to whom, as he offered solemn sacrifice at the altar, seven men of the clergy ministered. Ours was his Archdeacon Lawrence, whom the adversaries cast out of their calendar, to whom, twelve hundred years ago, the Consular man Prudentius thus prayed:

> What is the power entrusted thee,
> And how great function is given thee,
> The joyful thanks of Roman citizens prove,
> To whom thou grantest their petitions.
> Among them, O glory of Christ,
> Hear also a rustic poet,
> Confessing the crimes of his heart
> And publishing his doings.
> Hear bountifully the supplication
> Of Christ's culprit Prudentius.

Ours are those highly-blest maids, Cecily, Agatha, Anastasia, Barbara, Agnes, Lucy, Dorothy, Catherine, who held fast against the violent assault of men and devils the virginity they had resolved upon. Ours was Helen, celebrated for the finding of the Lord's Cross. Ours was Monica, who in death most piously begged prayers and sacrifices to be offered for her at the altar of Christ. Ours was Paula, who, leaving her City palace and her rich estates, hastened on a long journey a pilgrim to the cave at Bethlehem, to hide herself by the cradle of the Infant Christ. Ours were Paul, Hilarion, Antony, those dear ancient solitaries. Ours was Satyrus, own brother to Ambrose, who, when shipwrecked, jumped into the ocean, carrying about his neck in a napkin the Sacred Host, and full of faith swam to shore (*Ambrose, Orat. fun. de Satyro*).

Ours are the Bishops Martin and Nicholas, exercised in watchings, clad in the military garb of hair cloths, fed with fasts. Ours is Benedict, father of so many monks. I should not run through their thousands in ten years. But neither do I set down those whom I mentioned before among the Doctors of the Church. I am mindful of the brevity imposed upon me. Whoever wills, may seek these further details, not only from the copious histories of the ancients, but even much more from the grave authors who have bequeathed to memory almost one man one Saint. Let the reader report to me his judgment concerning those ancient blessed Christians, to what doctrine they adhered, the Catholic or the Lutheran. I call to witness the throne of God, and that Tribunal at which I shall stand to render reason for these Reasons, of everything I have said and done, that either there is no heaven at all, or heaven belongs to our people. The former position we abhor, we fix therefore upon the latter.

Now contrariwise, if you please, let us look into hell. There are burnt with everlasting fire, who? The Jews. On what Church have they turned their backs? On ours. Who again? The heathen.

What Church have they most cruelly persecuted? Ours. Who again? The Turks. What temples have they destroyed? Ours. Who once more? Heretics. Against what Church are they in rebellion? Against ours. What Church but ours has opposed itself against all the gates of hell? When, after the driving away of the Hebrews, Christian inhabitants began to multiply at Jerusalem, what a concourse of men there was to the Holy Places, what veneration attached to the City, to the Sepulchre, to the Manger, to the Cross, to all the memorials in which the Church delights as a wife in what has been worn by her husband. Hence arose against us the hatred of the Jews, cruel and implacable. Even now they complain that our ancestors were the ruin of their ancestors. From Simon Magus and the Lutherans they have received no wound. Among the heathen, they were the most violent who, throughout the Roman Empire, for three hundred years, at intervals of time, contrived most painful punishments for Christians. What Christians? The fathers and children of our faith. Learn the language of the tyrant who roasted St. Lawrence on the gridiron:

>That this is of your rites
>The custom and practice, it has been handed
>   down to memory:
>This the discipline of the institution,
>That priests pour libations from golden cups.
>   In silver goblets they say
>That the sacred blood smokes;
>And that in golden candlestick, at the nightly
>   sacrifices,
>There stand fixed waxen candles.

Then is it the chief care of the brethren,
As many-tongued report does testify,
To offer from the sale of estates,
Thousands of pence.
  Ancestral property made over
To dishonest auctions,
The disinherited successor groans,
Needy child of holy parents.
  These treasures are concealed in secret,
In corners of the churches;
And it is believed the height of piety
To strip your sweet children.
  Bring out your treasures,
Which by evil arts of persuasion
You have heaped up and hold,
Which you shut up in darkling cave.
  Public utility demands this,
The privy purse demands it, the treasury demands it,
That the soldiers may be paid for their services,
And the commander may benefit thereby.
  This is your dogma, then:
Give every man his own.
Now Caesar recognises his own
Image, stamped on the coin.
  What you know to be Caesar's, to Caesar
Give; surely what I ask is just.
If I am not mistaken, your Deity
Coins no money,
  Nor when he came did he bring
Golden Jacobuses[1] with him;
  But he gave his precepts in words,
Empty in point of pocket.
  Fulfil the promise of the words
Which you sell the round world over.
Give up your hard cash willingly,
Be rich in words.
        (*Prudentius, Hymn on St. Lawrence*).

[1] The Latin is Philippos.

Whom does this speaker resemble. Against whom does he rage? What Church is it whose sacred vessels, lamps, and ornaments he is pillaging, whose ritual he overthrows? Whose golden patens and silver chalices, sumptuous votive offerings and rich treasure, does he envy? Why, the man is a Lutheran all over. With what other cloak did our Nimrods[1] cover their brigandage, when they embezzled the money of their Churches and wasted the patrimony of Christ? Take on the contrary Constantine the Great, that scourge of the persecutors of Christ, to what Church did he restore tranquillity? To that Church over which Pope Silvester presided, whom he summoned from his hiding-place on Mount Soracte that by his ministry he might receive our baptism. Under what auspices was he victorious? Under the sign of the cross. Of what mother was he the glorious son? Of Helen. To what Fathers did he attach himself? To the Fathers of Nice. What manner of men were they? Such men as Silvester, Mark, Julius, Athanasius, Nicholas. What seat did he ask for in the Synod? The last. Oh how much more kingly was he on that seat than the Kings who have ambitioned a title not due to them! It would be tedious to go into further details. But from these two [Emperors, Decius and Constantine], the one our deadly enemy, the other our warm friend, it may be left to the reader's conjecture

---

[1] Seems to refer to the first Protestant bishops, *mighty hunters* (Genesis x. 9) after place, and, to secure it, all too ready to alienate the manors and possessions of their see.

to fix on points of closest resemblance to the one and to the other in the history of our own times. For as it was our cause that went through its agony under Decius, so our cause it was that came out triumphant under Constantine.[1]

Let us look at the doings of the Turks. Mahomet and the apostate monk Sergius lie in the deep abyss, howling, laden with their own crimes and with those of their posterity. This portentous and savage monster, the power of the Saracens and the Turks, had it not been clipped and checked by our Military Orders, our Princes and Peoples,—so far as Luther was concerned (to whom Solyman the Turk is said to have written a letter of thanks on this account), and so far as the Lutheran Princes were concerned (by whom the progress of the Turks is reckoned matter of joy),—this frantic and man-destroying Fury, I say, by this time would be depopulating and devastating all Europe, overturning altars and signs of the cross as zealously as Calvin himself. Ours therefore they are, our proper foes, seeing that by the industry of our champions it was that their fangs were unfastened from the throats of Christians.

Let us look down on heretics, the filth and fans

[1] I have here paraphrased, as any literal translation would have been hopelessly obscure to most modern readers. Campion could but hint darkly his comparison of the Elizabethan persecution to the Decian. The Latin runs: *Etenim, ut nostrorum illa fuit Epistasis turbulenta, sic nostrorum haec evasit divina Catastrophe.* *Epistasis* is "the part of the play where the plot thickens" (Liddell and Scott). *Catastrophe* is "the turn of the plot" (Id.).

and fuel of hell[1] the first that meets our gaze is Simon Magus. What did he do? He endeavoured to snatch away free will from man: he prated of faith alone (Clen. lib. i. recog.; Iren. l. I, c. 2). After him, Novatian. Who was he? An Antipope, rival to the Roman Pontiff Cornelius, an enemy of the Sacraments, of Penance and Chrism. Then Manes the Persian. He taught that baptism did not confer salvation. After him the Arian Aerius. He condemned prayers for the dead: he confounded priests with bishops, and was surnamed " the atheist" no less than Lucian. There follows Vigilantius, who would not have the Saints prayed to; and Jovinian, who put marriage on a level with virginity; finally, a whole mess of nastiness. Macedonius, Pelagius, Nestorius, Eutyches, the Monothelites, the Iconoclasts, to whom posterity will aggregate Luther and Calvin. What of them? All black crows,[2] born of the same egg, they revolted from the Prelates of our Church, and by them were rejected and made void.

Let us leave the lower regions and return to earth. Wherever I cast my eyes and turn my thoughts, whether I regard the Patriarchates and the Apostolic Sees, or the Bishops of other lands, or meritorious Princes, Kings, and Emperors, or the origin of Christianity in any nation, or any evidence of antiquity, or light of reason, or beauty of virtue, all things serve and support our faith. I call to witness the Roman Succession, *in which*

---

[1] *Faeces et folles et alumenta gehennae.*
[2] *Mali corvi.*

Church, to speak with Augustine (*Ep.* 162: *Doctr. Christ.* ii. 8), *the Primacy of the Apostolic Chair has ever flourished*. I call to witness those other Apostolic Sees, to which this name eminently belongs, because they were erected by the Apostles themselves, or by their immediate disciples. I call to witness the Pastors of the nations, separate in place, but united in our religion: Ignatius and Chrysostom at Antioch; Peter, Alexander, Athanasius, Theophilus, at Alexandria; Macarius and Cyril at Jerusalem; Proclus at Constantinople; Gregory and Basil in Cappadocia; Thaumaturgus in Pontus; at Smyrna Polycarp; Justin at Athens; Dionysius at Corinth; Gregory at Nyssa; Methodius at Tyre; Ephrem in Syria; Cyprian, Optatus, Augustine, in Africa; Epiphanius in Cyprus; Andrew in Crete; Ambrose, Paulinus, Gaudentius, Prosper, Faustus, Vigilius, in Italy; Irenaeus, Martin, Hilary, Eucherius, Gregory, Salvianus, in Gaul; Vincentus, Orosius, Ildephonsus, Leander, Isidore, in Spain; in Britain, Fugatius, Damian, Justus, Mellitus, Bede. Finally, not to appear to be making a vain display of names, whatever works, or fragments of works, are still extant of those who sowed the Gospel seed in distant lands, all exhibit to us one faith, that which we Catholics profess to-day. O Christ, what cause can I allege to Thee why Thou shouldst not banish me from Thine own, if to so many lights of the Church I should have preferred mannikins, dwellers in darkness, few, unlearned, split into sects, and of bad moral character!

I call to witness likewise Princes, Kings, Emperors, and their Commonwealths, whose own piety, and the people of their realms, and their established discipline in war and peace, were altogether founded on this our Catholic doctrine. What Theodosiuses here might I summon from the East, what Charleses from the West, what Edwards from England, what Louises from France, what Hermenegilds from Spain, Henries from Saxony, Wenceslauses from Bohemia, Leopolds from Austria, Stephens from Hungary, Josaphats from India, Dukes and Counts from all the world over, who by example, by arms, by laws, by loving care, by outlay of money, have nourished our Church! For so Isaias foretold : *Kings shall be thy fosterfathers, and queens thy nurses* (Isaias xlix. 23).

Listen, Elizabeth, most powerful Queen, for thee this great prophet utters this prophecy, and therein teaches thee thy part. I tell thee: one and the same heaven cannot hold Calvin and the Princes whom I have named. With these Princes then associate thyself, and so make thee worthy of thy ancestors, worthy of thy genius, worthy of thy excellence in letters, worthy of thy praises, worthy of thy fortune. To this effect alone do I labour about thy person, and will labour, whatever shall become of me, for whom these adversaries so often augur the gallows, as though I were an enemy of thy life. Hail, good Cross. There will come, Elizabeth, the day, that day which will show thee clearly which have loved thee, the Society of Jesus or the offspring of Luther.

I proceed. I call to witness all the coasts and regions of the world, to which the Gospel trumpet has sounded since the birth of Christ. Was this a little thing, to close the mouth of idols and carry, the kingdom of God to the nations? Of Christ Luther speaks: we Catholics speak of Christ. *Is Christ divided?* (1 Cor. i. 13). By no means. Either we speak of a false Christ or he does. What then? I will say. Let Him be Christ, and belong to them, at whose coming in Dagon broke his neck. Our Christ was pleased to use the services of our men, when He banished from the hearts of so many peoples—Jupiters, Mercuries, Dianas, Phoebades, and that black night and sad Erebus of ages. There is no leisure to search afar off, let us examine only neighbouring and domestic history. The Irish imbibed from Patrick, the Scots from Palladius, the English from Augustine, men consecrated at Rome, sent from Rome, venerating Rome, either no faith at all or assuredly our faith, the Catholic faith. The case is clear. I hurry on.

Witness Universities, witness tables of laws, witness the domestic habits of men, witness the election and inauguration of Emperors, witness the coronation rites and anointing of Kings, witness the Orders of Knighthood and their very mantles, witness windows, witness coins, witness city gates and city houses, witness the labours and life of our ancestors, witness all things great and small, that no religion in the world but ours ever took deep root there.

These considerations being at hand to me, and

so affecting me as I thought them over that it seemed the part of insolence, nay of insanity, to renounce all this Christian company and consort with the most abandoned of men, I confess, I felt animated and fired to the conflict, a conflict wherein I can never be worsted until it comes to the Saints being hurled from heaven and the proud Lucifer recovering heaven. Therefore let Chark, who reviles me so outrageously, be in better conceit with me, if I have preferred to trust this poor sinful soul of mine, which Christ has bought so dearly, rather to a safe way, a sure way, a royal road, than to Calvin's rocks or woodland thickets, there to hang caught in uncertainty.

CONCLUSION

You have from me, Gentlemen of the University, this little present, put together by the labour of such leisure as I could snatch on the road. My purpose was to clear myself in your judgment of the charge of arrogance, and to show just cause for my confidence, and meanwhile, until such time as along with me you are invited by the adversaries to the disputations in the Schools, to give you a sort of foretaste of what is to come there. If you think it a just, safe, and virtuous choice for Luther or Calvin to be taken for the Canon of Scripture, the Mind of the Holy Ghost, the Standard of the Church, the Pedagogue of Councils and Fathers, in short, the God of all witnesses and ages, I have nothing to hope of your reading or hearing me.

But if you are such as I have pictured you in my mind, philosophers, keen-sighted, lovers of the truth, of simplicity, of modesty, enemies of temerity, of trifles and sophisms, you will easily see daylight in the open air, seeing that you already see the peep of day through a narrow chink. I will say freely what my love of you, and your danger, and the importance of the matter requires. The devil is not unaware that you will see this light of day, if ever you raise your eyes to it. For what a piece of stupidity it would be to prefer Hanmers and Charks to Christian antiquity! But there are certain Lutheran enticements whereby the devil extends his kingdom, delicate snares whereby that hooker of men has caught with his baits already many of your rank and station. What are they! Gold, glory, pleasures, lusts. Despise them. What are they but bowels of earth, high-sounding air, a banquet of worms, fair dunghills. Scorn them. Christ is rich, who will maintain you: He is a King, who will provide you: He is a sumptuous entertainer, who will feast you; He is beautiful, who will give in abundance all that can make you happy. Enrol yourselves in His service, that with Him you may gain triumphs, and show yourselves men truly most learned, truly most illustrious. Farewell. At Cosmopolis, City of all the world, 1581.

THE END.

K

Milton Keynes UK
Ingram Content Group UK Ltd.
UKHW040859050124
435493UK00006B/936